Who from our Mother's arms...

BRISTOL TO BETHLEHEM

LYNN WEAVER

ISBN 0-948728-24-8

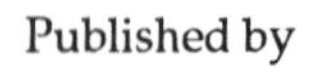
Published by

Friendly Press
300 Gloucester Road
BRISTOL BS7 8PD
England

Typeset by IN-HOUSE TYPESETTING, Brighton, England
Printed by SHORT RUN PRESS, Exeter, England

This Book is dedicated to
NELLIE SUMMERSCALES
who lit the spark of inspiration
to bring it into being.

Now thank we all our God,
with hearts, and hands, and voices,
who wondrous things have done,
in whom His world rejoices;
Who from our mother's arms,
hath blessed us on our way
with countless gifts of love,
and still is ours today...

CONTENTS

Foreword	vii
Chapter 1 Who From Our Mother's Arms	1
Chapter 2 "Mum & Dad"	4
Chapter 3 A Time and Season	8
Chapter 4 Feed My Lambs	13
Chapter 5 Earth Has Many A Noble City Bethlehem Thou Dost Excel	20
Chapter 6 Stablish—Strengthen—Settle You	30
Chapter 7 Hope School	35
Chapter 8 Bethlehem Bible College	50
Chapter 9 His Lambs	56
Chapter 10 Whoever Gives Up... Shall Receive...	69
Chapter 11 Thou Shalt Dwell In The Land In Safety	79
Chapter 12 A Piece Of Chocolate	84
Chapter 13 The Ways Of The Lord Are Right	91
Chapter 14 Christmas In Bethlehem	103
Chapter 15 The Lord is MY Shepherd	111
Epilogue	119

FOREWORD

Far too many books have been written on the Middle East — its conflicts, its antagonism, its wars, massacres, crusades, religious tensions and hatred.

Far too little has been written about people — yes, there is not just religion, politics and military: there are people, actual people; men, women, boys and girls, in the Middle East. But this is what God saw all the time: He saw people, He loved people. Jesus moved about people, good and bad, rich and poor. He was their friend, healer, feeder and ultimately their Saviour.

As long as we talk and read about armies, terrorists, intefada, moslim fundamentalism, holocaust and prophecy, we forget that **in** *and behind all this are people and to get close to them, any one of them, on both sides of the conflict, enables us to have influence on the above mentioned.*

I know that many of you who are now reading these words have been concerned, worried, at times angry or even confused when you saw the pictures on TV. You wondered how we could be of any help other than prayer — but the difficulty soon presented itself: ***how*** *to pray and for whom.*

But are we really forced to choose? Or is that human pressure the result of small thinking? The result of our very limited capacity to love? So that if we are **for** *one we are automatically* **against** *the other?*

As for myself: I refuse to choose. Rather I have chosen: for people. For justice. For peace which can only be based on justice. For sharing Jesus with people, ordinary people.

This lovely, charming and truly disarming book by my good friend Lynn Weaver shows us how to do just that.

Get personally involved, without choosing sides. Just go and find people, get close to them, listen — yes, above all else listen. Offer them your heart, your hand and your shoulder for them to cry on.

Just **be** *there. That is exactly how my own ministry began, almost 40 years ago. My very first trip was behind the "iron* *curtain" (a few more years and many will not even remember what that stood for) in a tightly controlled and, as far as the Church was concerned, rather restricted country.*

There, on my first visit to a church, the pastor said to me: "Andrew, your being here means more than ten of the best sermons."

I knew I could not preach (well), having just come out of the Missionary Training College — but I could be there. And if that meant more than 10 good sermons, why preach?

Just be there. Rub shoulders.

Almost exactly the same words were said only a few years ago in Beirut, Lebanon: "Andrew, when everyone is leaving, you come. That is the greatest encouragement we can get..."

And now read Lynn's story. Of bringing **hope** *in a seemingly hopeless situation. Lynn shows that you can* **do** *it. After all: she did it. And I hope she doesn't mind me saying: if Lynn did it you* **can** *do it.*

But first read this true story that will captivate you and carry you away to a level of Christian life that you always wanted to live yourself. Now you can see that it was not only George Muller, Hudson Taylor, Helen Keller or Corrie ten Boom but men and women who are alive today, showing to an unbelieving Church and a cynical world that we can **all** *have a part in changing the world by the way we live. Gloriously for Jesus.*

Not to mention the many other benefits: to see the Holy Land without paying the tourist price, to gain insight that reporters sadly miss, to have the greatest possible sense of fulfilment even in a life lived under stress, to find indeed Bethlehem's Shepherd's care for you personally.

I close to hear Jesus say — one day — "Well done, you good and faithful servant".

Well done Lynn. God bless you.

Brother Andrew

Chapter 1
Who From Our Mother's Arms

For John Arthur Dixon and Rose May Raynor, 29th July, 1939, was a very special day. A day to forget the threat of war which hung over Europe. A beautiful English summer day. Their wedding day. A day full of love. Their family and friends gathered together to share this special day with them and most of all their love for each other. A love that had blossomed slowly but surely over a period of many years and which on this day, they would affirm in the solemnisation of marriage.

As they stood in the Parish Church of St. John the Evangelist, Mansfield, in the County of Nottingham, they made their vows to each other before God. John, taking Rose's hand in his, declared — "I take thee, Rose May, to be my wife, to have and to hold from this day forward, for better, for worse, for richer for poorer, in sickness and in health, to love and to cherish, till death us do part, according to God's holy law, and this is my solemn vow." As he looked upon her with love in his eyes and listened as she made the same vows to him, little did he know that death would indeed part them and that she would be his wife for one precious year only.

Within a few days of their first wedding anniversary John found himself again standing in the same Church, this time with tears in his eyes and alone. No, not quite alone, for his beloved Rose had died in childbirth, leaving him with a tiny baby daughter. The baby was born at the Nottingham Hospital for Women in Peel Street, on Sunday 21st July 1940. She was very tiny and underweight and was placed in an incubator at the side of the Ward Sister's desk. Rose could see her little daughter, the child she had so desired, but she was unable to hold her close because she herself was fighting for her own life. John came to visit his wife and daughter with joy in his heart, not realising the seriousness of Rose's sickness and registered the baby as Rosalind Dixon. He left the hospital trusting he would soon have them both home with him. Rose and the baby received other visitors a few days later. John's sister Daisy and her husband James Weaver had both been present with Rose and John on their wedding day and James had been a witness to their signatures on the wedding certificate. Daisy was very close to her brother John.

Growing up had not been easy, the family was far from rich and often without food, though never short of the love and care of good parents. John was not strong physically and had suffered typhoid in his early teens. Daisy watched over him and saw he got extra food when it was available. In fact, he had a scar on his foot caused early one morning whilst he and Daisy were still children. Daisy had crept downstairs with him, put the frying pan on the coal fire and into it put fat and bacon to cook for his breakfast. They were huddled close to the fire to keep warm and the pan of hot fat tipped onto John's foot, leaving a scar which would always remind him of her love for him. A love that she would show over and over again.

Daisy also came to love Rose, the girl John chose for his bride and it was this love that brought her to visit Rose and the new baby in the hospital in Nottingham that July morning, in spite of it being war time and having to travel many miles to get to the hospital. Visiting time was restricted and as the Ward Sister rang the bell to tell the visitors it was time to leave, Daisy kissed her sister-in-law goodbye. As she walked away from the bedside Rose spoke words that in the coming weeks were to become embedded in her mind. Rose said, "Don't forget, you are to be my little girl's Godmother!" They were the last words she was to hear from Rose's lips for within days Rose's fight for life was over and John was left with his tiny daughter to care for.

For him the future looked bleak indeed but what of the baby, was she to be denied the love of a mother's arms just when she needed it the most? No, she was not denied that love. On the 28th August 1940, at just one month old, she was taken to the Church of St. John the Evangelist, Mansfield (in the County of Nottingham). This Church over the past thirteen months had witnessed the marriage of her parents and the funeral of her mother. There she was baptised Rosalind Dixon. She was held in the arms of Daisy Emily Weaver, who with her husband James, had agreed to be her Godfather and Godmother.

A few weeks after the Baptism Daisy visited her brother John, who asked her if she would be willing to become the little girl's adopted mother and once again she showed her love for her brother by saying yes. In spite of having 3 teenage daughters herself and caring for two girl evacuees from Lowestoft, she returned from the visit with the baby in her arms. She and her husband, James, then began the legal process of adoption in order to give the baby the same name and rights as their own daughters, Dorothy, Christine and Mary. The adoption certificate states:—

> *"It is ordered that James Weaver, who is by occupation a Coal Miner, and Daisy Emily Weaver, his wife, be authorised to adopt Rosalind Dixon and it is directed that the Registrar General shall make an entry and that the name of the said infant be entered as Rosalind Dixon Weaver."*

So it was that I became the fourth daughter of James and Daisy Weaver. Parents chosen for me by the gracious hand of God, who, from my natural mother's arms has indeed blessed me on my way.

Chapter 2

"Mum & Dad"

Not only did God give me the love of a new mother and father, plus three sisters, He gave me the added bonus of the love of my natural father. For I regularly visited him until his death in 1973 when I was 33 years old. He never remarried, living with my grandmother until her death in 1968 and then with my cousin Doris who looked after him from then on. What a privilege to have the love of three fathers — God, my heavenly Father; John, my natural father (always known to me as my Jackie whilst I was growing up and then as Jack); and James, my adopted father. Yes, my God, has blessed me on my way with countless gifts of love. His hand has been on my life from its beginning and in this and following chapters I will share His blessings and His leadings over the years.

My certificate of adoption says:—

> *"The Petitioners (James and Daisy Weaver) undertake to make for the said Rosalind Dixon the following provision, namely:*
>
> *'To maintain and educate her in a manner ordinarily considered suitable for a child of parents occupying the social position of your petitioners.'"*

The "social position" of Mum and Dad, as they soon came to be known by me, was not considered to be of much standing in those days. Dad on his 13th birthday began work at the Shirebrook Colliery, Derbyshire, where he remained employed as a coal miner for 52 years and the home they provided for me was owned by the Colliery. There was no electricity only gas lighting and then not even that in the bedrooms, we went to bed by candle light in winter. We had no bathroom only a sink in the scullery for washing, not only ourselves but the dishes, the vegetables, the clothes, etc. etc.

The toilet was outside next to the coal house and the coal fire range heated the room, the oven and the hot water. Mum made clothes for people and ran a club for a local drapery shop, going from house to house to collect the money people paid each week for the clothes they bought from the shop. But James and Daisy Weaver were special people and they gave me an education far above that considered suitable for a child of my social position. Mum had loved English at School, especially poetry and she passed that love on to all her daughters, reading to us and encouraging us to read for ourselves. Both Mum and Dad loved music and the theatre and we had a radio, gramophone and piano in our home. As I grew older I was taken to the ballet, to concerts and to the theatres in London. Nature was another love and Mum could name almost all the wild flowers that grew in the Nottinghamshire and Derbyshire countryside and she taught me the names as we walked as a family to the local beauty spots of Scarcliffe Woods, Pleasley Vale and Sookholme. They also had a great "social awareness" and cared deeply about people and willingly helped where they could, mostly unobtrusively. They took an active part in the Labour Party in the 1940s and 50s, both locally and regionally, feeling that by so doing they would be able to help the ordinary people in their struggle for a decent life style. Mum became Chairman of the Women's Section in our area and when I left the Model Village Secondary Modern School in our village of Shirebrook, she was appointed to the Board of Governors. However, their provision for me went far beyond education, they gave me something priceless.

At my baptism on August 28th, 1940, when I was one month old, they as my Godparents, undertook the following responsibilities —

To see that I was taught the Christian faith.

To see that I was brought up to attend the Services of God in His Church.

On my Baptism Certificate, which they signed, are the following verses:

"O ye who came that babe to lay
Within a Saviour's Arms today
Watch well and guard with careful eye
The heir of immortality.
Teach her to know a Father's love
And seek for happiness above
To Christ her heart and treasure give
And in the Spirit ever live.
That so before the judgement seat
In joy and triumph ye may meet
The battle fought, the struggle o'er
The Kingdom yours for ever more."

Yes, they did lay me in the Saviour's arms that day, but He gave me back into their arms knowing that He could trust them completely to fulfil their promises. They did indeed teach me, mostly by their own example, to know the Father's love and to seek for happiness above. *To Christ my heart and treasure I have given and in the Spirit I ever live.*

They are now with that Saviour, who laid me in their arms and I know that without a doubt one day:

"Before the judgement seat in joy and triumph we will meet,
The battle fought, the struggle o'er
The Kingdom ours for ever more."

As I was going through Mum's papers after her death in 1975, I found a note-book and on the front was written:

> ***D.E. Weaver*** *— this book is hers. Not to be read without permission given from one who has striven to collect and write verse and maybe to lead her thoughts to her Father, the good Lord in Heaven.*

She once said to me, "Lynn (the name the family called me with affection) I want you to know that whatever you do will be alright by me." So I took this as her permission to read the book and to include one poem she wrote about me:

GUARDIAN ANGELS

We often talk of Guardian Angels,
but know not of what shape or form they take,
or how they visit us.
But this I know without a doubt
They do not all have wings.
We took a baby girl when her mother died at birth.
She filled our lives with joy, no greater on this earth.
She had her guardian angel, with coat of dirty white,
except for patches here and there of black on ears and face.
Now Towser was a neighbour's dog,
A bulldog mastiff so they said,
I wouldn't know because about dog breeds I'm completely in afog.
I'll tell you all about him, if I may.
Each morning around nine o'clock
I'd glance through the window and there, as large as life he sat,
Waiting for me to wheel her pram outside, I'm sure he could tell the time.
Rain, blow or snow he would be there, sitting beside her pram
and woe betide anyone who dared to poke their heads beneath that hood.

He didn't even trust my husband to take her for a walk,
No matter where they went behind he'd softly stalk.
This thing about Towser was so uncanny,
He was far more attentive than a nanny.
Alas he died but not before
My baby had grown to a little girl.
We missed him so and loved him,
This Angel.

Chapter 3

A Time and Season

One of the recurring memories of my childhood and teenage years is of cold frosty Christmas Eves and going to the Midnight Service at the Parish Church of the Holy Trinity, in the village of Shirebrook on the borders of Derbyshire and Nottinghamshire. Our village got its name because the brook that ran through the village divided the Shires. During the service, when the carol "Oh Little Town of Bethlehem" was announced, Mum would look at me and smile. It was her favourite carol and she would often recall hearing a boy cousin, Jonty Weaver, singing the boy soprano solo of the opening verse. She would say "his voice was like a bell". Somehow that carol became "Christmas" for us, neither of us knowing that one day the Lord would call me to that little town of Bethlehem to serve him there. She would never know on earth for she went to be with her Saviour, three years before I first visited that little town.

As for me, looking back, that carol was the beginning of a desire to go to the Land of Jesus's earthly sojourn, to stand in the places He had stood in, just simply to be there. The desire was for no more than a visit, but He had other plans.

A favourite Scripture of mine is

"To everything there is a season and a time for every purpose under the heaven". Ecclesiastes 3

God's timing is not ours and His time for me to visit His land was not until I was 38 years old in 1978. The intervening years, though I didn't know it, were preparing me for God's purposes.

From my natural mother, Rose, I inherited a love of children. I was told that when she heard the song, "The little boy who Santa Claus forgot", she would say, "I wish I knew who he was, I wouldn't let him be forgot!" My older cousins have told me how much they loved Aunty Rose when they were little, she had a way with little ones and that was her gift to me. So at the age of 15, I began to train as a Nursery Nurse at the Violet Markham School, in Chesterfield. I qualified for the N.N.E.B. (The Certificate of the National Nursery Examination Board) in 1957 and immediately was employed as a Nursery Assistant at St. Lukes Church of England School, in Bedminster, Bristol. My older sister Dorothy had married Don (a Bristolian,) and made her home in Bristol so I went to live with them. Eventually my other sister Chris and her family came to live in Bristol and Mary, my third sister, married a Bristol boy and they emigrated to Canada. On Dad's retirement in 1961 he and Mum came to live with us in Bristol also and Bristol has been home base ever since.

From St. Luke's I was transferred to Filton Avenue Nursery School and enjoyed looking after the children there. My favourite age is two, in spite of it being known as the "terrible two's". It is so precious to have a little one slip their hand trustingly into yours or climb onto your lap for a story and through all my life God has graciously brought little ones to me to love. He has also used little ones to minister to me, especially in times of sadness.

During this period, my brother-in-law, Don, introduced me to Toc H an organisation born out of the First World War, whose main aim in a nutshell is "Practical Christianity". I was a member of the Shirehampton Women's Branch for over 15 years, attending weekly meetings and sharing the jobs the Branch undertook—visiting a Children's Home to sew and iron; taking round the supper time drinks at the Bristol Royal Infirmary; the shop trolley at the Homeopathic Hospital; the Library Trolley at Frenchay Hospital; visiting elderly people who lived alone; making up Christmas parcels of food for people in need and singing Christmas carols at Ham Green Hospital. Gradually I was given administrative jobs within the Branch and Area; Secretary, then Chairman, then District Team representative and finally Central Councillor. Not easy assignments for me as through my teens and early adulthood I struggled with shyness. However I came to realise if the Lord wanted me to do these jobs He would help me do them, and He did.

During 1962/63 I worked with my friend Pauline Illsley, as assistant house-mother in the Downend Children's home. We had 10 children to care for from the ages of 5 to 16 years, most of them from disturbed backgrounds and this gave me experience of older children and living in a residential situation.

In June of 1963 I went for an interview with the Post and Telecommunications and was accepted. So began 19 happy years doing clerical/secretarial work. After a few years I was assigned to the Welfare Department working with the Welfare Officers throughout the South West Region from Gloucester to Lands End. I loved the job for it included lots of organisation, arranging First Aid training and Competitions; Duke of Edinburgh Award Scheme for young people; Youth Camps; Pre-retirement Conferences and Welfare staff conferences. It also included lots of person to person situations, answering telephone calls from people in need of help and "looking after" the Welfare Officers themselves! We worked as a team and it was a rewarding time.

The first Welfare Officer I worked closely with was Juliette Durham and she became a spiritual mother to me. She was President of the Post Office Christian Association and soon had me going to the meetings and eventually I became the Secretary. It was much more than a meeting to me, through the speakers and fellowship with Juliette I received real spiritual food and grew much in my Christian walk.

When the family had settled in Bristol I began attending St. Andrew's Church, Montpelier and it was like being part of an extended family. I joined the Choir and there, for the first time I became a Sunday School teacher. When St. Andrew's was closed in 1964 several of the congregation joined St. Nathanael's, Cotham and there too I became involved in the Sunday School. In the autumn of 1975, Rev. Ray Brazier with his wife, Elizabeth and daughters Ruth, Debbie and Helena, came to minister at the Church and with their coming my walk with the Lord began to be a living relationship. Elizabeth's father, Canon John Radford and his wife Rita, held a Renewal Mission at the Church and the Holy Spirit began to work in many lives, mine included.

With Ray and Elizabeth's encouragement, I with other helpers started a Pathfinder Group for boys and girls age 10 to 16. We had a Club night once a week and a Bible Study on Sunday mornings and lots of activities including camping weekends and joining national Pathfinder camps. It was a time of giving and learning, a special time indeed for me.

So it seemed to me the pattern of my life was set. A job I enjoyed, a home I shared with my family, involvement in the work of my Church, holidays abroad, a good lifestyle. Yet deep within me was a space — a restlessness — something I wasn't sure of — a yearning perhaps? It was difficult to define but I felt there was something more for me.

My desire to visit the Holy Land was still with me and I had made two attempts to get there. In the early 1970s I had applied to go as a volunteer for a month with a group going to the Edinburgh Medical Mission Hospital in Nazareth but as most of the group were in their teens I was considered to be too old! So I waited and in the December 1974 CMJ Magazine I saw a tour advertised for May 1975. I applied and was accepted. However, that was not to be either, for on 1st January 1975, Mum was taken ill with leukaemia and within six weeks had gone to be with her Lord. So I put thoughts of going on one side until one winter evening early in January 1978. I was sitting on the floor in the Church Hall, surrounded by Pathfinders, when a dear friend, Phyl Bryant, walked into the hall. She shared my desire to go to the Holy Land and as she walked over to me she said, "Brian Treharne, from Christ Church, Cotham, is taking a tour to the Holy Land in May. Would you come with me?"

Would I!

The door had opened for my heart's desire and I was definitely going to go through it this time.

A holiday of a lifetime? No, the experience was going to change my whole life for not only would I see the sites, I would have an encounter with the risen Lord and eventually I would return to the Judean Hills to the little towns of Bethlehem, Beit Jala and Beit Sahour and begin the work the Lord had been preparing me for all these years.

Chapter 4

Feed My Lambs

Brian Treharne and his wife, Chris, who were leading the tour wrote:

> JERUSALEM & THE HOLY LAND —
> THE JOURNEY OF A LIFETIME
>
> "It is impossible to convey in words the sheer excitement of one's first visit to the Holy Land, scene of the life and ministry of our Lord. The Gospel takes on a new dimension as one re-lives the events in Jerusalem, where time seems to have stood still for millennia. From scores of memorable experiences I'll select just one. On the journey from Judea to Galilee we stop and drink from the well of Sychar, where Jesus revealed to the woman of Samaria that He is the living water which can slake the thirst of all mankind.
>
> Refreshment of body, mind and spirit are assured and the benefits in increased awareness and understanding of the Bible are, for the Christian, invaluable. We have carefully chosen the dates for our visit, 27th May — 6th June, 1978, to ensure least crowds and most equable climate. Why not join us and make 1978 the year you will never forget?"

Prophetic words? For me, yes! 1978 is the year I will never forget — it was my time to "fall in love". Not with the Holy Land itself, but with my Lord and Saviour, Jesus Christ. For as He revealed Himself to the woman at the well of Sychar so He revealed Himself to me. Not in a tangible way but deep within until I knew I had found "The pearl of great price" and the one indelible memory I brought back with me from that "tour" was the knowledge that Jesus Christ is alive indeed.

Another member of the tour brought back a souvenir of that journey of a lifetime. It was a video she had taken as we travelled the Land and I played the star role in one of the scenes she shot. It was early one morning just after daybreak, when a group of us left the hotel (the Pilgrims Palace, near Damascus Gate) where we were staying. We took taxi cabs to the top of the Mt. of Olives and then walked down the narrow pathway that Jesus came riding on the donkey on that first Palm Sunday. As we neared the Garden of Gethsemane, at the foot of the Mt. of Olives, around the corner came a young Arab boy with his flock of sheep and goats. He was riding a donkey and had a palm branch in his hand. Seeing a group of English tourists his re-action was quick. Here was a chance to make a few shekels by having his photograph taken with them. He jumped off the donkey, threw down the palm branch and picked up the tiniest lamb in his flock. He walked up to me, placed the lamb in my arms, put his arm around me and stood with a big grin on his face. A happy holiday memory? Or was it something more? It was definitely something more. For on my return the Lord began to lead me in so many different ways.

> *"So when they dined, Jesus saith to Simon Peter, son of Jonas, lovest thou Me more than these? He saith unto Him, 'Yea, Lord, thou knowest that I love Thee.' He saith unto him, 'Feed My lambs.'"*
>
> *John 21 verse 15.*

It would be nearly four years before I knew which lambs the Lord wanted me to feed and during those four years I would once more return to the Holy Land for a tour. I believed that would be my last visit to the Land of the Bible, never dreaming that God intended me to live there.

The first tour had lasted ten days and each day was crammed with so much to see that it was almost too difficult to take it all in, especially whilst in Jerusalem. Our first day there we drove to the top of the Mt. of Olives, visited the Church of Ascension then walked to the Paternoster Church where Jesus taught the Lord's Prayer, then stopped at

Dominus Flevit Church where Jesus wept over Jerusalem and on to the Garden of Gethsemane. We then piled into the coach and drove to Bethlehem passing Rachel's Tomb. Next we visited the Nativity Church in Manger Square, walked up to the Souk (the open air market) and then on to Beit Sahour and the Shepherds Fields, where the angels appeared to the shepherds announcing the news of the Messiah's birth. Back into the coach to ride up to Bethlehem, stopping at a souvenir shop to see the olive wood carvings and mother of pearl made by the local Palestinian Arabs.

All this before lunch and then not even time for a quick nap before we were off again. This time to see the Model of Jerusalem at the time of the Second Temple and the Dead Sea Scrolls. Back into the coach to the Old City and the Pool of Siloam where Jesus healed the blind Man. We were allowed to stop for a drink of freshly squeezed orange juice before setting off again to see St. Peter Gallicantu, the site of Caiphas the High Priest's house. This was where Jesus was taken after His arrest and where Peter denied Him. Finally we ended up on Mt. Zion to see the Tomb of David and the Cenacle, the second floor room marking the site of the Passover meal Jesus shared with His disciples.

I was so confused by the end of the day that it wasn't until I had returned to Bristol and made my scrapbook of the tour that it all fitted into place. "Wouldn't it be lovely", I thought to myself if I could go back once more and take a more leisurely look at the places. As I shared memories of my visit, several friends told me they had also longed to make a visit to the Holy Land and would I be willing to join them on another tour? Again I was to get my heart's desire.

This time the tour leaders were Derek and Margaret Cleave from Christian Ministries. The dates for the tour were 31st May to 14th June, 1980. A longer period and more leisurely than the first one and I was just as awestruck to be going as I was the first time. The flight was from Heathrow airport so my friend, Jane and I caught the train to Reading and then to Heathrow. As we made ourselves comfortable in the second train I saw a lady in the compartment who had an identification badge like ours pinned to her coat. We had been asked to wear them so we could link up with the rest of the group at the airport. We introduced ourselves and she said she was also from Bristol and that her name was Elsie Isaacs. That was the start of a beautiful friendship, which was to last until Elsie's death in June 1992. Neither of us were aware that our coming together was planned by the Lord and that we would participate in a special occasion which would bond us. Like me this was also Elsie's second visit to the Holy Land and the Lord was taking us back for His purposes.

After we had settled into the hotel (the Y.M.C.A. situated opposite the King David Hotel), we met together with the group to discuss the programme and get to know one another. Derek, the leader, said as he closed the meeting, "Incidentally, someone in the party has asked for baptism in the River Jordan when we visit there on the 9th June. If there is anyone else who would like to be baptised I will be happy to arrange it."

The next morning as we were waiting for the coach to take us sight seeing, Elsie approached me and said, "Lynn, I am the one who is going to be baptised, have you ever thought about being baptised by total immersion? I would be so happy if we could both be baptised together in the River Jordan."

Elsie, who I had only met the day before, was a total stranger to me and the only one out of a group of 35 people to approach me about baptism. How did she know that over a period of time the Lord had been challenging me about this subject? Yes I had received infant baptism and yes, I had been confirmed at the age of 12; though the one memory that remained in my mind from that occasion was that I had to wear grey shoes because my parents couldn't afford to buy me a pair of white shoes like all the other girls wore. Wasn't that sufficient? The Lord seemed to be saying "No" and was gently, slowly nudging me to take the step of baptism by total immersion. The next few days of the tour were overshadowed by an inner turmoil as I struggled with the decision I knew I had to make. I enjoyed once again visiting the places in

Jerusalem and the surrounding area but deep within I was remembering the Scriptures and books and friends the Lord had been using to bring me to this moment. The book "Appointment in Jerusalem" by Lydia and Derek Prince was the main challenge. In particular Lydia's own experience and the chapter entitled "The Burial" in which she finally underwent Baptism by total immersion. Her feelings were of a deep, settled peace and the thought "that she had done what God required of her."

Then there was my own longing and desire to publicly acknowledge that Jesus was my personal Lord and Saviour.

> *"Know ye not, that so many of us as were baptised*
> *into Jesus Christ, were baptised into His death.*
> *Therefore we are buried with Him by baptism into*
> *death,*
> *that like as Christ was raised up from the dead by*
> *the glory of the Father,*
> *even so we also should walk in newness of life."*
>
> *Romans 6 verses 3 & 4*

Within me was a strong feeling that I wanted to be dead to sin, I wanted the burial of my old way of life. I wanted to be buried with Jesus by baptism. As Jesus was raised up from the dead so I wanted to be raised to a new life with Him. I wanted it, but was I sure that God wanted it also? That was my question to Him as I knelt in prayer on the night of 5th June 1980. The next morning before I got out of bed, I opened my Daily Light and there read:

> *"Lo, a voice from heaven, saying. This is my*
> *beloved Son, in whom I am well pleased."*
>
> *Matthew 3 v 17.*

The account of Jesus's own baptism. It was God the Father's wish that His beloved Son go through the waters of baptism and His beloved Son was obedient. It was God the Father's wish that His beloved daughter, Rosalind, also go through the waters of baptism and she too would be obedient.

So it was that a group of British pilgrims scrambled down the bank of the river Jordan at Deganya (there was no official baptism site in 1980 like there is today) on a lovely June morning to witness the baptism of Elsie Isaacs and Rosalind Dixon Weaver. The hymn, Amazing Grace, was chosen and as Elsie walked into the water where Derek Cleave waited to baptise her, the first verse was sung. As she walked out, the second verse was sung and then I stepped into the cool green water of the Jordan and walked towards Derek. The group sang the third verse:

Through many dangers, toils and snares
I have already come,
Twas grace that led me safe thus far
And grace will lead me on.

Then followed the immersion into those cool waters and as I went under the words were ringing in my ears, "*I baptise thee, in the name of the Father, Son and Holy Spirit.*" I surfaced and walked back to the shore with a feeling of being clean all over, inside and out, and with a peace in my heart that passed understanding. Later in the day the thought came to my mind; "God does have a sense of humour, in July I will be 40 years old and they do say life begins at 40!"

I was to find God had something else in store for me in that 40th year. He was to give me something to equip me for the rest of my walk on earth with Him.

As I returned to Bristol and took up my life there once again, caring for Dad who was now 84, doing my job with British Telecomm, leading the Pathfinder Group at St. Nathanael's Church, I found something had changed within me. I was unsettled, restless and not knowing why. Looking back I realise the Holy Spirit was at work in me, sifting me, preparing me and equipping me. One of the first things I did on my return from the Holy Land was to read and study all the references in the Bible concerning Baptism. I wanted to know what it was I had experienced that June morning at the River Jordan. One passage of Scripture that challenged me was the account of Peter and Cornelius in Acts Chapter 10. Especially the last five verses (44 to 48).

"While Peter yet spake these words the Holy Ghost fell on all them which heard the word. And they of the circumcision which believed, were astonished, as many came with Peter, because that on the Gentiles also was poured out the gift of the Holy Ghost. For they heard them speak with tongues and magnify God.

Then answered Peter, Can any man forbid water, that these should be baptised, which have received the Holy Ghost as well."

Again I realised, that over a long period of time, the Lord had been nudging me to seek not only water baptism but the baptism of the Holy Spirit as well. He had brought me into relationships with Pentecostal friends, He had challenged me through Chris Cameron (nee Rostron) at Pathfinder Camp and through Dennis and Rita Bennett's book "Nine O'Clock in the Morning". Again I had reached the point where I wanted to receive the Baptism of the Holy Spirit and again I had to be absolutely sure that God wanted it. Once more I knelt in Prayer. "Father, do You want me to receive the laying on of hands for Baptism in the Spirit?" The answer I received was again from Daily Light. The portion for the evening of September 18 contained the following Scriptures:

"En-hakkore or the well of him that cried.
If thou knewest the gift of God who it is that saith to thee, Give me to drink, thou wouldest have asked of Him and He would have given thee living water.
If any man thirst, let him come unto to Me and drink.
This spake He of the Spirit, which they that believe on Him should receive.
Prove Me now herewith, saith the Lord of Hosts, if I will not open you the windows of heaven and pour you out a blessing,
that there shall not be room enough to receive it.
If ye being evil, know how to give good gifts unto your children, how much more shall your heavenly Father give the Holy Spirit to them that ask Him.
Ask and it shall be given you, seek and ye shall find."

Monday, 22nd September, 1980, I knelt at the altar rail of St. Nathanael's Church, Cotham, Bristol. The Rev. Ray Brazier anointed me with oil and then laying his hands upon my head, asked the Lord to baptise me in the Holy Spirit. There were others kneeling at the altar rail that evening to receive the laying on of hands for healing. When all had been prayed for, we returned to our seats, set in a circle, to praise the Lord. As I sat there just two words came into my mind, words that to me made no sense — Aramantha, Parthanon. I recalled that in Dennis and Rita Bennett's book they had said no matter if the words didn't make sense, it was our job to speak them, so I did over and over again. Later, when I had returned home, I went to my room and sat in my chair. Those two words filling my mind, then came the thought "sing them" and as I began to sing, other beautiful words and melodies came pouring forth and I sat for over two hours worshipping and praising the Lord in my new language. Gradually over the coming months as I spent time in prayer and reached the point of not knowing how to continue I began to pray with words not from me, again words I didn't understand but which seemed to express all I wanted to say to the Lord. Then during the house-group meetings I was part of in St. Nathanael's Church, in our time of prayer a stillness would come over the group and I knew that I had to pray in my new language, a quiet peaceful language like a gently flowing river. Then I would pray in English, words of blessing, assuring us of God's love and encouraging us in our walk with Him.

I had asked and been given the gift of Baptism in the Holy Spirit. There was one more question the Lord was waiting for me to ask, "Which lambs do You want me to Feed, Lord?" I waited five more months until February 1981, before finally asking and as always He answered me but I wasn't so sure this time that I liked the answer.

Chapter 5

Earth Has Many A Noble City Bethlehem Thou Dost Excel

Christmas, 1980, had come and gone. Carol sheets put away for another year, thoughts of Bethlehem and the birth of Christ receded as thoughts of the New Year ahead filled my mind, what would 1981 hold for me? Back into the routine of home, work and church activities after the festive season and coping with the winter weather seemed to make life a one day at a time business with a "let the future take care of itself" attitude. Until the 21st February dawned, bright and clear. I, as normal, was walking down Stokes Croft to my office in Mercury House, Old Market, Bristol.

The week before I had gone to the mid-week Bible Study at Church and the Vicar, Ray Brazier, had asked us to turn to John 21 in our Bibles. There it was again, verse 15, Feed My lambs. In my inner being, and almost in desperation, I cried out to the Lord. "Alright Lord, I am willing to feed Your lambs, but You will have to show me which lambs You want me to feed."

Here I was, one week later, going about my normal business, walking along one of the busiest roads in Bristol at 8.15 a.m. when into my mind came an Epiphany hymn, "Earth has many a noble city, Bethlehem, thou dost excel". Bethlehem, Bethlehem, Bethlehem... like an old fashioned gramophone record with the needle stuck, that one word was with me all day long as I answered the telephone, typed letters, made tea and coffee, walked home, had supper with Dad, until finally I went up to my room, sat in my chair and quieted myself. There in the stillness my eyes focused on two things. The first was a poster on the wall of bread and wine. "Bethlehem in Hebrew, means House of Bread", I thought to myself. The second item that caught my attention was a little book on my bedside table, which had been sent to me for Christmas. The title of the book was, "Come Home" and the picture on the front was of a flock of sheep. Bethlehem, the Shepherds Fields! "Lord do You really want me to go to Bethlehem"? "No I can't be hearing You right. I don't want to go to Bethlehem". Those were the thoughts that tumbled round and round as I sat there, trying to take in what I thought I was hearing. A few days later I got out the atlas to see if there were any other Bethlehems in the world. There are but in the evening of Saturday 21st March, 1981, I knew without a doubt that it was Bethlehem, Ephrath, David's City, that the Lord wanted me to go to feed His lambs.

The house was quiet, my father and I sat by the fire reading. I picked up the book of Bible Readings used in my Church to read the Scriptures which would be read at the Church Services the next day, Sunday, March 22nd. I didn't get beyond the first verse —

> *"The Lord said to Abram, 'Leave your native land, your relatives and your father's house and go to the country that I am going to show you.'"*
>
> *Genesis 12 verse 1*

I knew that the Lord was saying to Rosalind Weaver, "Leave your native land of England, your relatives and your father's home in Bristol and go to the city I have already shown you — Bethlehem." I closed the book sharply and as I did so my sister, Dorothy, whose home Dad and I shared, opened the door of our sitting room and said, "Haven't you got the television on? There is a lovely programme about Israel on BBC2". I went cold and very reluctantly asked my father to turn on the television. We were just in time to see the end of the programme, the author, Amos Oz was seated on the grass, surrounded by a group of children telling them a story.

The next morning I went to Church in a dream and as I sat in the congregation I looked around at all my friends and thought to myself, "I don't want to leave my father's home, I don't want to leave my family, I don't want to leave my friends." The rest of the day passed with my mind in turmoil until it came time to go to bed. Before I switched off the light I thought to myself, "Don't worry, it will work itself out. Just read Living Light and go to sleep." I opened Living Light to read the portion for the evening of Sunday 22nd March and this is what I read:

> *"You will need the strong belt of truth and the breastplate*
> *of God's approval.*
> *You will need faith as your shield to stop fiery arrows*
> *aimed at you by Satan.*
> *And you will need the helmet of salvation and the*
> *Sword of the Spirit, which is the Word of God.*
> *The Lord is with you.*
> *I will make you strong.*
> *Go... I am sending you."*

"But I can't just go to Bethlehem", I heard myself saying, a few evenings later, as I shared with Ray and Liz Brazier. "I don't know anyone in Bethlehem and for my father's sake I have to know where I am going." "Right", said Ray, "Start knocking on doors and if you are meant to go the right door will open."

Back home, alone in my room, I was thinking whose door do I knock on and I thought of three organisations who had ministries in the Holy Land.

The Bible Lands Society, through whom I had sponsored Houson, a spastic girl at the Four Homes of Mercy in Bethany.

CMJ — The Churches Ministry to the Jews, who I knew had several different ministries in the Land.

Prayer for Israel and Ken Burnett, whose prayer letters I received.

So began the process of sharing with these groups and a time of waiting for their response.

I had finally accepted that God did indeed want me to go to Bethlehem and that I had no choice in the matter, except to be obedient. Each morning as I walked to work I had to wait at the traffic lights at the end of Newfoundland Road in order to cross the road and as I stood there, the National Coach to London, would go through the lights. I knew beyond a shadow of a doubt, that one day I would be seated on that coach on my way to the airport — to catch the flight to Tel Aviv — on my way to Bethlehem. What I would be doing there or where I would be living was still a mystery known only to the Lord who was sending me there.

I received replies from the Bible Lands Society and CMJ, understanding replies but regretfully they were unable to help me find "my place" in Bethlehem. Then I received a fat package from Ken Burnett, Prayer for Israel. The package contained all the information for working on a Kibbutz with a lovely letter from Ken, suggesting I complete the applications. Before signing off Ken added one last sentence. "If you still feel it is Bethlehem you are being called to, we have heard of a Bible College which has just opened in Bethlehem. If you would like to write to them we will see they get the letter."

Once again I approached the Lord, "If you want me to write this letter please let Bethlehem come up each day for a week and I will write at the end of the week". This was July, 1981, even in England the shops don't prepare for Christmas that early! Yet at the end of the week Bethlehem had indeed cropped up each day in the hot July weather.

1. Bamber Gascoigne on University Challenge asked the competitors to name three people who had lived in Bethlehem.

2. A friend's mother had died and as I was looking in my box of cards for a suitable condolence card I found a card with pressed flowers from Bethlehem.

3. A Bible reading in Genesis said, "Jacob buried Rachel on the way to Ephrath (Bethlehem).

4. The Sunday School class were doing jigsaws and one child called me over to see the one she had chosen, the Manger Scene in Bethlehem.

5. The Bible Lands Society Magazine had an article about the Lutheran School in Bethlehem.

Finally at the Friday evening Pathfinders meeting something happened that left me in no doubt that I was to write a letter to the Bible College in Bethlehem. I arrived early at the Church Hall to prepare the room. One of the Pathfinders, Sarah Febry, arrived shortly afterwards. She said she had come early as it was her turn to play the hymns on Sunday morning and she wanted to practise them. I gave her the hymn numbers and over to the piano she went. As she began to play the second hymn I stopped dead in my tracks, walked over to the piano and said, "Sarah, why are you playing that hymn?" "Because that's the number you have given me", she said. I looked at the list. No, I hadn't given her that number but I knew why she was playing it. It was the Calypso Carol, "Come now, carry me to Bethlehem".

"Alright Lord, You don't have to carry me, I will go on my own two feet, of my own free will. I will write this letter to the Bible College. I don't know who I am writing it to so I'll address it 'Dear Brothers'. I will tell them that You want me to come to Bethlehem but I don't know what You want me to do there. I will tell them that I am a qualified Nursery Nurse and a Secretary and ask them if they know of anyone who could use me. Then I will wait for their answer."

The airmail letter I received in reply, was dated August 17, 1981. It was signed by Solomon Douhne, Headmaster Hope Secondary School and by Alex Awad, Acting President, Bethlehem Bible College. It said:

"Greetings in the Name of our Lord and Saviour, Jesus Christ.

Miss Christie from the Sunday School Store in Jerusalem gave us your letter. (I learnt later that Ken Burnett had sent my letter to Aviva Tiller in Jerusalem who had then passed it onto Miss Florence Christie who in turn passed it on to Alex Awad!) We read your letter carefully and we are praying that God will lead you according to His purpose.

We are writing on behalf of Hope Secondary School and Bethlehem Bible College. Let us explain to you the possibilities of working at both places. At Hope School there is a need for a secretary to co-ordinate all sponsorship programs. There is a possible need of someone to teach English to Arab speaking students. At the Bethlehem Bible College we could use a secretary to work on transcripts and correspondence. At present neither the Hope School nor the Bible College can support a secretary. If the Lord opens the door for you to come our way you must come as a volunteer. The Hope School, however, can provide for you free room and board.

Before we can accept your request we need the following:

1. A letter of recommendation from your pastor.

2. A letter of recommendation from your former employer.

3. A letter from you stating your willingness to serve with us as a volunteer.

4. If at all possible we prefer to have a personal interview with you or with someone who knows you very well.

As a general requirement we expect our workers to be called by God to this ministry, to love the Lord and love the people (Arabs) with whom they minister.

Feel free to write or call and let us keep in touch until we see how the Lord directs.

Signed,

Solomon Douhne, Hope Secondary School Alex Awad, Bethlehem Bible College"

My reply was as follows:

"Greetings to you in the Name of Jesus, our Lord and Saviour.

Thank you for your letter of 17 August and for your prayers that God will lead me according to His purpose. That is my own prayer too.

Thank you for so clearly explaining the possibilities of work at Hope School and Bethlehem Bible College.

I think I am able to meet your 4 requirements.

I have a friend, who is a Christian and with whom I have worked for many years. His name is Allan Dodd and he and his wife, Peggy, will be going to Jerusalem on 25 October for 3 days so if the Lord leads then, they will be able to meet with you on my behalf."

My friends Allan and Peggy Dodd duly visited the School one afternoon during their tour of the Holy Land in October 1981 and reported back to me. Their general impression was that I was needed and that I would be warmly welcomed. They weren't sure exactly where I would live. Allan thought it would be in a large room at the School used for storing books, he didn't think there was a window in the room! Peggy quickly assured me he'd got it wrong, yes it was used for storage but it was light and airy and definitely had a window! They also shared that Solomon and Alex thought it would be good if I had a driving licence so I could drive the School and College Minibus. That was one thing I didn't possess, never ever having a desire to drive nor having a need to. Allan also said that they felt it would be necessary for me to meet the Committee before they could make a final decision to accept me.

Again another letter winged its way from Bristol to Bethlehem and I explained that I didn't drive but would be willing to learn but that this would take quite a time if I were to do it in England. I also said I would be willing to make the necessary visit to meet the Committee.

Christmas 1981 came and went and still I waited for a reply to my letter. Finally it arrived dated 23 January 1982 with an apology that it had been overlooked in the Christmas activities and vacation. The letter then went on to say:

"We appreciate your further correspondence with us and feel led to welcome you at any time. The Bible College will have facilities available so that you can stay there. Since the building is located close to Bethlehem, you do not have to over worry about driving, but can commute by bus, private car etc. It is also a short walk to the Nativity Square in Bethlehem. We are in need of a Secretary at the Bible College and will find your services needful as soon as possible.

We realise that you are still seeking the Lord and we trust God to help you make the right decision. We are excited with the work and look to God for furthering of His Kingdom.

May your life be filled in all abundance with the blessings of our Lord.

In Christian love,
Solomon Douhne and Alex Awad"

So it seemed that the time had at last come for me to board the London Coach on the first stage of my journey to Bethlehem, but it wasn't quite time for me to begin my work there. I had one weeks holiday left for the 1981/82 holiday period and so I decided to use it to visit the Hope School and Bethlehem Bible College, trusting that the Lord would show me clearly that this was where He wanted me. I wrote to Solomon and Alex telling them of my intention of coming and received a telegram saying:

> "WELCOME, WILL TAKE CARE OF ACCOMMODATION, TELL US WHEN ARRIVING".

I telephoned to say I would be arriving on 22nd April and welcomed I was. As I pushed my trolley out of Ben Gurion Airport, wondering who had come to meet me and how I would recognise them, I spotted a man in the crowd holding a large piece of card which said, "WELCOME, LYNN WEAVER." "That's me", I said as I walked up to him and he introduced himself as Alex Awad, Acting Principal of Bethlehem Bible College. (His brother Bishara, the Principal was in the U.S.A. for a year of study.) With Alex was his six year old daughter Christy and they drove me to Hope School to meet Solomon, his wife Sue and children, David and twins Stephanie and Stephen. Solomon is a Syrian Arab and Sue is American, they met at Lee College in Tennessee. Alex and Christy then took me to their home in Beit Sahour to meet Brenda and two year old Basem. Alex is a Palestinian Arab and Brenda is American. They, like Solomon and Sue, met at the Church of God, Lee College in Tennessee. I was to spend the week in their home and what a week it proved to be. Not only did the Lord show me so clearly that He did indeed want me at Bethlehem Bible College and Hope School but He drew Brenda, Alex, Solomon, Sue and I together as true brothers and sisters in Him.

One special incident happened that left me in no doubt that not only was this the place the Lord wanted me but that He loved me very much and would meet all my needs.

One warm April afternoon during my stay, Alex asked me if I would like to go with him to visit an American family who lived in Beit Sahour. They were returning to the U.S.A. and selling all their furniture. Alex and Brenda were buying their carpets. So I said "Yes" and off we set. We had a very pleasant visit, drinking orange juice and sharing. I told them I would probably be coming to work at the Bible College and Hope School as a volunteer. We prayed for their little girl who was sick and then loaded the carpets in the car and waved goodbye. Alex and I got into the car and we were just pulling away from the kerb when the husband ran down the path and through the open window thrust a beautiful red rose into my hand saying, "We want you to have this". I didn't even have time to say thank you as Alex drove off. I sat gazing at the rose then I noticed something wrapped around the stem. Unrolling the piece of paper I found it was a $100 bill. Alex quietly said, "That is definitely from the Lord. That family do not have that kind of money to give." On our return to the house I showed Brenda the rose and dollar bill and asked her if I could borrow her salon (the room kept for guests in an Arabic home) for a while as I wanted to be alone with the Lord. "Of course you can", she said, "But the Lord is only showing you He is going to take care of you".

Yes He was and yet He was saying so much more than that. As I sat enjoying the rose and its perfume it came to me that when a man loves a woman he gives her flowers, usually red roses. He gives her perfume and he gives her gifts. My Lord Jesus was showing me so clearly how much He loved me and that I needn't worry about the future. I was in the place He wanted me to be in and He would meet my every need.

Settled in my mind that I was to work at Bethlehem Bible College and Hope School, I returned to Bristol to begin the task of serving my notice with British Telecomm, handing over my Pathfinder Group and preparing my family for the moment I would leave them. The hardest part of all was leaving my father. He had asked if I couldn't wait until he had gone as he was now in his 87th year. When I gently shared that the Lord wanted it now, he lovingly accepted it and my older sister Dorothy said, "We don't want you to go but we know you must. We will take care of Dad."

One of my preparations was to try and get a driver's license by undertaking an intensive driving instruction course with the view of taking my test after 5 days. I gave up at the end of the third day and on arrival in Bethlehem I was not sorry I had given up. There was no way I could have coped with the Arab and Jewish drivers.

On the first day back at my office after the week's visit to Bethlehem a colleague in another section called me to ask if I would have lunch with her. Over coffee she gave me an envelope and said it was not from her but the Lord. When I got back to my desk and opened the envelope I found a cheque for £300. This was to occur over and over again until my departure on 29th June, people gave me envelopes containing different amounts of money. My Church which was then St. Nathanael's with St. Katherines, decided to support me for my first year.

There remained one more event to participate in before once again boarding the London coach en route to Bethlehem to begin the task of "Feeding His Lambs" and that was my commissioning by the Rev. Ray Brazier in the presence of the St. Nathanael's Congregation, my friends and my family.

The opening sentence chosen was:

> *"Jesus said, 'You did not choose Me but I chose you to go and bear fruit—fruit that will last.'"*
>
> *John 15 v 16*

The readings chosen were:
Acts 4 v 8-12 Faith in the Name of Jesus
John 21 v 15-19 Feed My Lambs.
The closing hymn:

Go forth for God...

Chapter 6

Stablish — Strengthen — Settle You

Fairy tales often finish in the middle of the story, the Prince finds his Princess and they live happily ever after. Life, fortunately I suppose, isn't like that. I had found the lambs God wanted me to feed and I was on my way to feed them. Even before I got there I learnt that it was not going to be a "bed of roses" all the way.

I arrived at Luton airport well in time for check in and was waiting in the departure lounge ready to board the plane at 11 a.m. I was still in the departure lounge at 5 p.m. and finally boarded the plane at 6 p.m. for take off at 6.15 p.m. Two planes had arrived for our flight only to be found unsafe to fly. The third plane proved to be air worthy! I had managed to get a message to Solomon at Hope School to say I would be late in arriving but when I finally arrived at Tel Aviv at midnight, I found no one waiting for me. I telephoned the School but no one answered. A friendly Jewish taxi driver said he knew Beit Jala and would take me for so many dollars. As I had checked in at Luton early that morning, my niece Tina, had given me an envelope which she said I was to open on the plane. Inside was a little note of encouragement and enough dollars needed for the taxi fare. So I got into the taxi and we set off, arriving in Beit Jala with no problem. Finding Hope School however, was a different story. I had only been to the School about three times during my week there and in the daylight. This was 2 a.m. in the morning with no one around and we got hopelessly lost. Finally I told the taxi driver to take me to the Police Station in Manger Square, thinking I could stay there until the morning. As I walked into the building I saw huge cockroaches walking all over the floor and I shuddered. However the Border Policeman on duty was friendly and helpful and with the help of the taxi man carrying my luggage, the policeman accompanied me to a little hotel at the side of the Church of the Nativity, called the Palace Hotel and rang the doorbell. The proprietor opened the door and welcomed me in. The border policeman said he would call for me at 8 a.m. to take me to the School. The taxi driver remonstrated with him and said that was too early, "Can't you see she is tired", he continued, "She's been travelling all day let her sleep until 10 o'clock"!

It was true, life wasn't going to be a bed of roses but I had learnt a very important lesson that night, the Shepherd who had called me to help Him feed His lambs was my Shepherd also and He would be with me all the way.

Inside the Palace Hotel I was shown into a single room with its own shower and toilet and the proprietor graciously assured me he would wake me at 8 a.m. for breakfast. Having checked that there were no cockroaches in this room, I lay on the bed and awaited the morning, anxious to be on my way to the School. At exactly 8 o'clock there was a knock on my door to tell me breakfast was ready and I was shown into the dining room, with apologies for the ladders and dust cloths covering everything, for the room was being repainted. In the middle of this huge room one table was laid and there I sat in solitary splendour, being the only guest in the hotel, to eat my breakfast.

The border policeman did not arrive and so I telephoned the School and within ten minutes Solomon was there with the School mini-bus and at last I arrived at Hope School. This time, not just for a few days but to stay, for as long as the Lord wanted me there.

It was decided that I would work Monday to Thursday at the School and Friday and Saturday at the Bible College in Bethlehem. Sunday being my day of rest. Accommodation for me, it seemed, was not so easy to arrange. The School Board, who ran the School, felt it wasn't fitting in an Arabic culture for a single lady to have a room in the School buildings, as there were 50+ boarding boys and their house-fathers, plus a male American volunteer also sleeping in the school. So the store-cupboard (which later would become my office) was not to be my home. There was a room at the Bible College available which overlooked the Shepherds Fields. As yet they had no solar panels for hot water and so for the time being it was decided that Monday to Thursday (whilst I was at the School) I would sleep at the Headmaster's house with the Douhne family, sharing a bedroom with the four year old twins Stephen and Stephanie and 9 year old David. Then over the weekends I would live with the Awad family (Alex, Brenda, Christy and Basem) in Beit Sahour and not far from the Bible College. Their house had a spare room which I could use. Although this was not an ideal situation it had the advantage of enabling me to get to know the local people who came to visit and be introduced to the culture and way of life of the Palestinians. Also as Brenda and Sue were Westerners like me, we were able to help and encourage one another.

Settling in wasn't easy, there was new food to get used to. Rice as the main meal most days, plus olives/pitta bread/immlukria (a kind of spinach)/tea without milk but with at least 2 spoons of sugar and mint/falafel (ground chickpeas made into small balls and fried in oil)/hummous (a paste of chickpeas and sesame seeds)/goats cheese and yoghurt/Arabic coffee (thick black coffee with ground cardamom added) and at the School the famous Mennonite meat — tins of ground beef or beef chunks sent to us by the Mennonite Central Committee and of course warak duwhali/koosa mashi and malfouf-stuffed vine leaves/courgettes and cabbage respectively/needless to say stuffed with rice and a little meat. There was the hot July weather to adjust to and a strange language ringing in my ears, one which I would have to try to learn in order to communicate.

In my Daily Light reading of July 31st, just one month after my arrival, I read the following Scripture:

> *"The God of all grace, who hath called us unto His eternal glory, by Christ Jesus, after that ye have suffered a while, make you perfect, stablish, strengthen, settle you."*
>
> *1 Peter, Chapter 5 v 10*

I got out my dictionary to look up those words and read:

Perfect: *complete not deficient; trained or skilled in duties; thoroughly learned.*

Stablish: *to set up; ordain (to admit to ministry); establish by decree or law; to destine.*

Strengthen: *to become or make stronger.*

Settle: *to become fixed or permanent; sink as a sediment; settles to free from uncertainty.*

In my own mind I could never see myself being perfect, stablished, strengthened and settled but then I wasn't being called to do it myself. It was the God of all grace who would make me be these things.

One of my first priorities was to find a place of worship and on my first Sunday with Alex and Brenda they asked me which Church I would like to go to. They would be quite happy to take me to one of the two Anglican churches in Jerusalem if I wished. "Where do you worship?" I asked them. "At the Church of God on the Mt of Olives", they replied. My next question was "Is the service in English?" "Yes it is, the Pastor is Martin Kielwein and he is German, his wife Veky is Yugoslavian and it is a Pentecostal Church but the service is in English!" Alex assured me. "Then I will go with you", I said. After the service I knew I had found my place of worship. What I didn't know was that I had also found a precious brother and sister in Martin and Veky and also in Gabi; Martin's sister who was a Church of God worker sharing the ministry; **plus** a place to live.

After I had been attending the Church about three months, Martin came to visit me and asked me if I would like a room in the Arabic Church of God in Beit Jala, with my own bathroom and use of the kitchen. The building, which was only built in 1980, was owned by the Yeteem family. Naim and Jeanette were known to everyone as Abu and Imm Basem. In Arab culture the birth of a son is very important. So much so, that when the first son is born his parents from then on are known by his name. Naim and Jeanette's first son was named Basem and so they became Abu (the father of)

Basem, and Imm (the mother of) Basem.

The building they owned had been purpose built for the Church but also had two apartments for local Palestinian families. The Church part of the building contained the Church meeting room; two Sunday School rooms; a youth meeting room and a spare room at the back adjoining the main bathroom. This was an added luxury with a bath plus shower and beautifully tiled in tan and brown. There was also a smaller bathroom and a kitchen with a balcony. Both Abu Basem and the Church of God were happy to have someone to live on the premises and I was more than happy to be that someone. The building was light and airy and the view from my bed/sitting room and kitchen looked over Bethlehem with Herodian in the distance. Herodian is a man made mountain built by King Herod and inside the mountain are the remains of one of his palaces. The balcony looked down onto a garden containing olive trees, apricot trees, grape vines, pomegranate trees and a huge Sabre plant (a giant cactus which has big orange fruit which can be eaten after all the prickles have been cut off, a job I left to the expertise of Imm Basem). This then was to be my home for the next ten years.

What I also didn't know was that it was in the little Arabic Church of God, pastored at that time by Solomon, that I was to find the special lambs God wanted me to feed.

Chapter 7
Hope School

Hope School, Al Amal in Arabic, is situated on top of one of the highest hills in Judea with views overlooking Jerusalem, Bethlehem and Ein Kerem, where John the Baptist was born. The valley at the back of the school is terraced and fertile with many fresh water springs and local tradition has it that it was a valley of giants.

The school buildings were originally built as a hospital but never used for that purpose and the family who owned them gave them to the Orthodox Charitable Society of Beit Jala to be used for the benefit of the town. In 1962 the buildings were leased to the Mennonite Central Committee who started a school for boys aged 12 years upwards. Most of the students were boarding students but some came daily. The Mennonite Central Committee ran the School until 1971 when they decided to hand it over to the local Palestinian Arabs.

Bishara Awad, was the School Principal at that time and he agreed to continue as Principal and formed a Charitable Society to oversee the running of the school. This meant the School would have to become totally self supporting as the Mennonite Central Committee gradually withdrew. Not an easy undertaking but Bishara and his wife Salwa, with their three children, Sammy, Samir and Dina, devoted the next 11 years to caring for the students at the school. Some were orphans, many with only one parent and the majority from poor homes. Bishara's own background had given him a strong desire to help these boys.

In Bishara's own words he says, "At the tender age of nine, in 1948, I watched as my father was shot in front of our house." Bishara's family lived not far from Damascus Gate in Jerusalem. Bishara continues — "My mother carried him inside the house and we had to bury him in the courtyard. Hatred began to fester inside me and when our home was then taken from us, it mushroomed into bitterness as I grew older." Bishara and his six brothers and sisters were put in orphanages and his mother, Huda, returned to nursing in order to support the family. Bishara goes on to say, "All the bitterness and hatred changed when as a young man I had a life changing encounter with Jesus Christ. This put a new perspective on life and I decided to pour my whole life into bringing God's love into the lives of my own people. Returning to the West Bank from the U.S.A. (after completing my education), I became Principal of Hope School Beit Jala, an orphanage school like the one I was brought up in. As I looked at these young boys, many in the same position as I had been, I didn't want them to grow up with the hatred and bitterness I had known and I dedicated my life to sharing God's love with them."

In 1981 Bishara decided to relinquish the Principal's position, though he remained on the School Board and continued a care and concern for the school. He had decided to work full time at the Bethlehem Bible College, which had been started on a part time basis a few years previously. The Lord had given him a vision for the College and it seemed a natural continuation of the School ministry.

Rev. Solomon Douhne, was appointed to take Bishara's place as Principal and came to the school in 1981. Solomon's own mother had died when he was a little boy in Syria. At sixteen years old and with little education he came into contact with the minister of a Church in Darra. The minister, who was blind, had been forced to leave his Palestine homeland several years earlier. Solomon got on well with the Pastor and was able to lead him around the town on his visits to people. It was through this Pastor that Solomon learned about Christ and became a new person. Solomon got work in an orphanage in Beirut and then went on to the Church of God Bible College in Switzerland. Eventually he went on to Lee College in the U.S.A. and there he obtained two degrees. He met and married Sue, whilst at the College and they set up home in Indiana and became teachers. They settled into the American way of life and had three children. Then Solomon began to have a distinct urge to return to the Middle East.

Solomon had met and formed a strong bond of friendship with Alex Awad, Bishara's brother, at the Church of God Colleges in Switzerland and U.S.A. and so Alex, who was teaching at Hope School then, suggested that Solomon be asked to become Principal of the School.

I arrived to begin work at the School, just one year after Solomon and so it seemed the Lord had His workers in position for the time being. Solomon as Principal of Hope School; Bishara as President of Bethlehem Bible College; Alex as Dean of students at the Bible College and me as the English Secretary of both the School and College. However there was one more member needed to make the team complete. George Shawrieh who arrived in September of 1982. George, to me, is a shining example of all that Hope School and Bethlehem Bible College stand for. He, himself had been a student at Hope School. His father was unable to work and so his mother had to bear the load of providing for six children, three girls and three boys. George and his two brothers, Oheh and Roni, came to the School and also their youngest sister Nuha. For gradually girls were allowed to come to the school as day students. George was the oldest and on his graduation from Hope School decided to enrol as a full time student at Bethlehem Bible College. After he had completed two years of study at the College he was awarded a Scholarship for one year to Christ for the Nations College in Dallas, Texas. It was at the end of this year that Hope School needed an Arabic Secretary/Administrator and so George was asked to consider the job. He was well qualified because the curriculum of Hope School included a course on business administration and secretarial studies. Life in the U.S.A. for a young Palestinian man was very different from his life on the occupied West Bank and it was a big temptation for George to stay in America. However, George decided to pray about it and finally telephoned to say he would return and accept the post because he knew the Lord wanted him to serve his own people.

Romans 5 verse 5 tells us,

"Hope maketh not ashamed, because the love of God is shed abroad in our hearts by the Holy Spirit, which is given to us."

That to me is what the ministry of Hope School was all about. God had placed His love in our hearts and through His Holy Spirit enabled us to pass on His love to the boys and girls which He placed into our care. For Hope School was more than a place of learning. It was home to 50+ boarding students and for all the students (day and boarding, boys and girls) it was the place where they heard the good news that Jesus Christ died for each one of them.

The school day began at 7.30 a.m. in the Chapel with a hymn of praise of worship, a short Bible reading or message and a time of prayer. Then it was down to the business of learning — Arabic; English; Maths; Science; Geography; History; Social Studies; Art; plus for the students aged 15 and over, typing in Arabic and English; Computer Science; Business studies including Book keeping and Secretarial skills. Lunch was at 1.30 p.m. for the boarding students and afternoons were taken up with various activities. For those who needed it, reading in the library with extra tuition from the librarian/teacher Sawsan Ghawali. Letters written to sponsors; football or basket ball; gardening or helping look after the chicken farm; playing table tennis or table games. Once a week there was the Stamp Club and twice a week the Christian Club for students who wanted to study the Bible, learn Christian songs and take part in quizzes etc. There was no school on Friday or Sunday as a third of the students came from Muslim homes. On Fridays the boarding students would sweep and clean the playground and tidy the area around the school. Then after lunch each student would have a shower and be given clean clothes from the house-mother. It was only one shower a week because the water was expensive to buy. During my last two years at the School the boys were able to go swimming at the Centre of the Bethlehem Arab Society for the Physically Handicapped. This was a great treat. On Sundays the Christian students would go to Church in the morning and then for a walk in the afternoons with the housefathers and Mennonite Volunteers.

The criteria for accepting students at Hope School was social and economic and most of the students fitted into one or more of the following categories; Orphans, or from one parent families or poor and needy. All were Palestinian Arab children. Whilst I was at the School there were only two true orphans, but we had many students whose fathers had died or been killed or left the family to live and work abroad. Some of the day students came specifically to learn the Business Studies programme and were from normal family backgrounds. None came from rich homes for the economic situation and the occupation makes it hard to make a living. Of course the students had to take an aptitude test to ensure they could cope with the academic programme but coming from the backgrounds they did, the majority found studying hard.

It was my job to prepare a case-history for each student which I sent to sponsors around the world. In the 10 years I was at the School, the Sponsorship Scheme expanded from World Vision and Mennonite Central Committee Sponsorship to include individual sponsorship from Friends of Hope School in England; U.S.A.; Canada and Iceland. Plus sponsors in Australia; Sweden; Holland and Germany.

The sponsor received a newsletter telling them the history of their student, a photograph, letters, Christmas cards and school reports. I got something much more precious for I knew the students themselves and was able to watch them change and grow, especially those who came at 12 years old and stayed until they were 18. Some blossomed, others got bogged down in the situation, all got despondent, frustrated and angry at having to live under occupation. For many this meant having to carry an I.D. card all the time; being constantly stopped by soldiers on the way to School; sometimes being hit by them or having their School books taken and burned for no reason. Not knowing if school would be open or not, either because of strikes which were aimed at highlighting the situation or by being closed by the army. In 1989 the school only managed 65 full days of teaching in the whole year. We overcame that by duplicating lessons and taking them to the students once every two weeks, bringing back their question papers for marking.

The students got to know that my office door was always

open and many found their way there for a variety of reasons — to bring me my tea and sandwich at the 10 o'clock break; to ask if I had any foreign stamps; if there was a letter from their sponsor or for help with their English or typing lessons. Some came to share their problems and for prayer, especially the handicapped students. Some came to help me put the newsletters into envelopes and stick on the stamps; others came to type letters for me as part of their typing course. Some came to give me gifts — a key ring made out of cork; a heart carved from the bark of a pine tree growing in the school grounds, with my initials on it. Others brought cakes made by their mothers for special Feasts and many came to share their mid morning snack with me. Some came to share their grief, particularly Rami, one young boy whose mother died of cancer when he was about 10 years old and then when he was 14 his father collapsed and died of a heart attack. For several weeks after the funeral he would come in his free time, with his stamp album and stand as close to me as he could get and spend his time sticking his stamps in and occasionally asking me the name of a country on a stamp until gradually he was able to join again in the football and games with his school friends. Abir was another who came for comfort after her 10 year old brother was shot and killed by soldiers because he threw a stone at them. Several students came unable to carry on with their lessons when they heard that one of the students (14 years old) had been shot at close range by soldiers, the rubber bullets taking part of his nose and ear away. As we prepared the 1990 Christmas letter, the students helping me decided to put a twig of olive in each letter and so out they trouped to pick branches from the olive trees. It was a time consuming job but they wanted to send a sign of "Peace" because deep down in each of their hearts, peace is what they long for. Peace to live their lives in freedom; peace to live in the homes their families have lived in for centuries; peace to study and make a future for themselves; peace free from the injustice of having land taken from them; of having their homes taken or blown up. Peace to enable them to travel freely, not abroad but just from village to village and to

Jerusalem and to their School.

It was not an easy task caring for the students but God had put His love in our hearts and very soon after my arrival He shared His love for them with me by showing me that they were Palestinians loved of God and that Hope School was one way of showing His love. He showed His love in so many ways, protecting the students from harm, enabling the School to remain open when other schools were closed and by providing, financially and materially, the necessities to feed, clothe and educate over 100 students; plus providing the salaries for the teaching staff and lady workers. All of whom, with the exception of Mennonite volunteers who served a 3 year assignment, were Palestinians.

Yes, God supplied, as He usually does, through people. For He planted His love in the hearts of His followers around the World for the students of Hope School.

The Mennonite Central Committee continued their support not only by sponsorship but by sending us a shipment every two years. The shipment contained enough cans of Mennonite beef to feed the boys for the two year period plus school bags containing note books, pens, pencils, rulers, erasers, and health kits — bags containing toothbrush, toothpaste, soap, flannel (washcloth to my American friends) comb and nail clippers, sheets, towels, pillowcases, lovely patchwork quilts, warm winter coats, underwear, pyjamas, shoes, sweaters and many other things. They also provided top soil so we could make a vegetable garden, and helped us buy a minibus tax free.

World Vision not only sponsored students but provided finance to rebuild the library after the water came through the roof, helped us to build another chicken house and what for me was a big help, they provided a photocopying machine.

The Canadian Embassy purchased new typewriters for the students plus IBM computers for the computer room.

Save the Children Fund installed a new sewage system.

Bible Lands Society completely renovated the kitchen and helped with purchasing chickens and paying towards the new toilet/shower facilities designed to take wheelchairs.

Christian organisations in Sweden and Holland also helped in many ways.

Catholic Relief provided flour, sugar, oil and helped with a large grant towards the new bathrooms.

From 1981 to 1987 each summer, **Teen Mission International** sent teams of teenagers to work at the school. They built a chicken house, a storage building, terraced the grounds, built pathways and completely wire fenced the whole of the grounds, a blessing in disguise for when the Intefada started it gave the school protection.

Locally, the baker supplied us with bread from the flour we gave him and Solomon's vision for a chicken farm proved to be a big contribution when all three houses were in operation. The farm was run by one of the teachers, Nimmer Butros, with the help of students. As well as providing the school with eggs we were able to sell to local supermarkets and local people. Handals the bakers in Bethlehem are noted for wonderful cakes and these cakes were made with Hope School eggs.

One of the biggest needs was the salaries for the teachers and the six ladies — Imm Salim the Housemother, Imm Jeries and Imm Hanna the cooks and later Im Kamal, Imm Wakeem the house-keeper, Imm Mustafa and Imm George who kept the school clean. In the ten years I was at the school no teacher or worker ever went without their monthly salary. The way it came was often miraculous and definitely in answer to prayer. As Solomon, George and I established ourselves as a team one of our first priorities was to set aside a time for praying together. We would thank the Lord for His provision and share our needs with Him. George and I continued this with each new Principal that was appointed. For, after 2 years, Solomon and Sue returned to the U.S.A. to take up their jobs which had been kept open for them.

Issam Hssen (a graduate of Bethlehem Bible College) took over from Solomon. Together with his wife Riet, from Holland and their two daughters Suzanna and Helene, they soon won their way into my heart. I got to grow close to the girls for while they were at the School, Riet lost the third child she was carrying and needed to have rest. Finally Suzanna and

Helene had another baby sister and she was named Marianne-Lynn. After serving two years, the family left the school, but by now Suzanne and Helene had a baby brother called Jonathan and Aunty Lynn got to look after the girls until he was brought home from hospital. It was during this time, after much prayer, I decided to work full time at Hope School. The work load was growing and needed my full attention.

For a while it wasn't certain who the next Principal would be but after much heartsearching and prayer Alex decided to leave the Bible College and take on the task. The two years Alex and Brenda were at the school were special years for me, made more so by the birth of their third child Randy Alex. My Dad went to be with the Lord on 13 November 1984 and I came home for the funeral and for Christmas that year. Whilst I was in Bristol I received a telephone call to say Brenda had given birth to a boy, so I was anxious to see him as soon as I returned. I took one look at him and it was "love at first sight"! He was 7 months old when he came to live in the School house but it wasn't long before he was finding his way into my office and once he had celebrated his first birthday and could walk, that was it. He wanted to come and help me everyday. One of my treasured moments from that period was when Randy was two and a half years old. George Shawrieh and I had to go into Bethlehem on School business, Brenda was busy and so I said I would take Randy for the ride. As he held my hand walking to the minibus, he looked up at me and said, "Where are you and me going, are we going to heaven today?" "No", Randy, I replied, "only as far as Bethlehem." I did caution George to drive carefully but as I thought on his remark I came to the conclusion that it would be a nice way to go to heaven, holding Randy's hand!

It wasn't time for that yet but it was time for me to be parted from Randy, his Mum, Dad, sister and brother. Alex had to leave the Land. For over a year he had been having problems getting a work permit and visa. Although he was born in Jerusalem and his family were all Palestinians he had been studying at the Church of God Bible College when the War of 1967 took place and so was out of the country. This meant he had lost his Palestinian status. He was able to obtain U.S.A. citizenship but when he came to his homeland to work amongst his own people at the Bible College and Hope School he had to come as a foreigner and obtain a visa and work permit. In 1987 after much representation on his behalf by the American Consulate, Jewish friends as well as Christian organisations, he was told he would have to leave the country. Fortunately he was accepted at the Asbury Theological Seminary to study for his M.A. which he later gained. He then planned to return to minister at the Arabic Baptist Church in Jerusalem and lecture at the Bible College. He travelled alone to prepare the way for Brenda and the children but he was only allowed to stay a few weeks and has not been allowed to return since. This was a big loss not only to me but to the students at the School and Bible College and for the Palestinian community for they have lost a man of God, a man of peace.

The year 1987 was to be the year for another parting, one I didn't expect and one that I found hard to come to terms with. Earlier in the year my three sisters suggested we get together at the home of Mary our sister who lived in Toronto. The suggested date was July and although the air fare from Tel Aviv to Toronto was high, Mary and her husband Mike, said they would help me with the fare. In May I got a message to say the date had been changed to September. "That means I can't go", I said to Alex, "School starts in September and I have all the case-histories to prepare." "Well you will have to wait until the students have all arrived and settled in first before you can begin the case-histories and it would be good to have you around in the summer with the Youth Camps etc. go ahead and plan to go in September," was Alex's reply. A few days later we received a letter from a gentleman who had visited the School at Easter, Albert Sankarlal. Albert wrote, "On my return to Canada I couldn't forget my visit to Hope School and have been sharing about it with several friends. They would like to help but wondered if they could meet someone from the school before committing themselves. Is there any chance that anyone from Hope School could come to Toronto in September?"

So not only did I get to visit with my family but I ended up speaking at the Holiday Inn, Etobicoke, about Hope School and Bethlehem Bible College and before my return the Rev. George Derkatch and his wife Diane, the Rev. Don Cuff and his wife Ida, and Albert and his wife Sylvia (all involved in the Evangel Bible Translators Ministry) had agreed to include Hope School and Bethlehem Bible College as part of their ministry. The Hope School family was growing. The support in Canada was later taken over by Hope Evangelistic Outreach with Allan Waddell taking care of the administration with a team to help him which included two Arabs living in Toronto, Nizar Shaheen and Rev. Shukri el Masri.

As well as speaking at the Holiday Inn I was able to go sight seeing with my family and of course Niagra Falls was a must. It was a lovely autumn day and the Falls looked beautiful in the sunlight. Mary, my youngest sister, remarked that she had seen the rainbow over the Falls many times but today it looked brighter than she had ever seen it. We each had our photograph taken under the rainbow. The rest of our time went quickly and we all prepared to return to our own places. Chris was the first to leave and then it was my turn. As I was saying goodbye I asked them to pray for my journey and that I would have no problem with re-entry. Dorrie my oldest sister always said to me that if I had to leave the Holy Land for any reason then there would always be a home for me with her and Don, her husband. This time she looked at me and said, "Well Lynn, if they don't let you in, you have lots of friends in England." Before I could respond the car was at the door to take me to the airport and as we pulled away I turned to wave to my two sisters. Those were the last words I was to hear from Dorrie's lips for on her return to Bristol she went to bed to catch up on sleep after the journey and never woke up on earth again. She suffered a severe brain haemorrhage and was in hospital for a month before leaving this earth behind. I flew home the day before the funeral and was able to view her body but my heart was troubled and upset at losing her.

Early on the day of the funeral my brother-in-law Don, Tina my niece and I went to early morning communion in a

Church near our new home. The family had moved to a smaller house when Dad died. The service was in the Lady Chapel and I went into the pew first. As I sat next to a stained glass window my mind gradually took in the details and I noticed the Scripture engraved on the window — John 14 verses 1 & 2, "Let not your heart be troubled, ye believe in God, believe also in Me. In My Father's house are many mansions..." At the funeral service, Rev. Ray Brazier spoke about "Rainbows". After the Service I asked him why he had thought about rainbows. "It just seemed right" he said but no longer was my heart troubled for I knew Dorrie was at peace in the Father's house.

Returning to Hope School I found it hard to settle, having lost Mum and Dad and now Dorrie, was something I found hard to adjust to but there was one of my new families in Beit Jala who needed my help just then.

After Alex and Brenda left a new Principal had to be found and again after much prayer the Lord provided. Not someone who was completely new to the School for the Lord brought Solomon back. He and Sue had returned a year earlier to Pastor the Church of God in Aboud. They now had four children, David, Stephen and Stephanie plus one year old Angela. So it wasn't like getting to know someone from the beginning.

The next few years were going to prove very difficult for life at Hope School but God was with us, helping and strengthening and protecting.

In December of 1987 the Intefada began. Intefada in Arabic means, uprising or throwing off the yoke. The Palestinian Arabs on the West Bank and Gaza Strip had reached a point where they could take no more. One incident proved to be one too many. Four young Palestinian Arabs driving in a car in Gaza were killed by an army patrol and the tension snapped and the desire to be free from military occupation and have a homeland of their own was in the open.

For the school this meant more closures by the army plus curfews being imposed. Not a curfew at night but a 24 hour curfew and it wasn't easy keeping 50 boarding students occupied inside the confines of the school building. Restriction of movement was frequent, often residents of the West Bank were not (and still are not) allowed into Jerusalem, which meant it was difficult getting the boys to their villages for the monthly weekend break or holidays. Strikes were called (and still are) in protest over young Palestinians being shot and killed. Some weeks we were only able to have one days schooling. All schools now had to finish at 1 p.m. and shops closed at 1 p.m. also. Teachers who lived the other side of Jerusalem had to obtain travel permission each month. Yet in spite of all this the School continued and God provided more and more financial and material support.

A new year dawned and was to prove very hard going. In February, Sue (Solomon's wife), was not well and after a visit to the doctor was admitted to Haddassa Hospital for surgery — she had cancer. Solomon had no family around him and the children wanted to stay together and so I became "Mum" for a month and yet another two year old worked her way into my heart, Angela. Mornings were spent doing the office work and the rest of the day and weekends spent looking after the children.

Mother's day on the West Bank always falls on 21st March and so it was celebrated whilst I was caring for the children. At the Sunday morning service at the Church of God on the Mt. of Olives pots of primulas were provided for the children to give their Mums. After the service, Stephanie and Stephen took a pot each and then came up to me. Stephanie said, "You're our Mom now, so this one is for you." Stephen then showed me his plant and said, "We will take this one to Mommy in hospital but I guess God wanted you to be our Mom now, so you could have a present as well."

Sue's own mother came from Indiana to look after her and then the whole family returned to the U.S.A. Solomon continued to be Principal of the school spending time between the school and the family but it was very hard for him. He kept going in this way until early 1990 but had to return to the family as Sue's health became worse and finally she went to be with the Lord in November 1990. (Solomon recently remarried and so the children have a new Mom of the Lord's choosing.)

I have always looked on Hope School and the sponsors as one big family and the family continued to grow in the years 1988–1992. I was able to visit England in the summers and travel around the country sharing about the School and College and in April 1991 I went to Iceland. This was at the invitation of Olafur Johannsson, a close friend of Solomon, the School, the College, and myself. Tour groups from England, Iceland, U.S.A. and Canada visited the School as part of their travels and my time was divided between office administration and a kind of public relations.

I came to England for the summer of 1990 and returned to find someone new sitting in the Hope School Principal's chair. Not just one person but two, for this time the Lord had brought a "joint Principal". Brice Brenneman and his wife Lydia. They were an ideal couple for the job. Brice is an American Mennonite and Lydia (nee Kuttab) a Palestinian Arab born in Bethlehem but raised in the U.S.A. Brice had a teaching degree and Lydia a degree in school psychology and would you believe it they had two little boys, Jonathan 2 years and Jameel 2 months!! Could my heart expand a little further to let in two more little ones, of course it could!

Brice and Lydia were ideal in more ways than one and together with George Shawrieh and myself we became a closely knit team. The welfare of the students and the staff being our goal.

Lydia's role was to co-ordinate the house keeping side of the school, planning menus, doing the shopping, supervising the ladies, sorting out the store cupboards of clothes, bedding and food supplies. As well as teaching English and expanding the library programme, she developed the monthly birthday party for the boarding students by including games which the boys loved and brought staff and students together in a closer family relationship. Brice, together with Lydia, approached agencies in the land and persuaded them to help financially with the Computer project, the Chicken Farm and the new bathroom/shower facilities. He also persuaded all the Mennonite community in Ohio and district to become sponsors or so it seemed to me for the list of U.S.A. sponsors tripled overnight! Jonathan and Jameel joined in everything and got themselves loved by everyone. Jameel developed into a creature of habit and each morning he would walk into my office and say, "Lynn, Lynn, boo". Boo being the Arabic children's word for a drink. Then he would point to my swivel typing chair and when I had sat him in it he would wait patiently for his drink, usually of hot chocolate.

Both Brice and Lydia, together with Erlis Miller the Mennonite Volunteer, spent many hours driving the students to their homes for the monthly breaks and feast celebrations. During the Gulf War they took food to the students in their homes under curfew. Having American passports meant they could move around freely.

One thing Brice introduced me to was "The Andy Griffith Show" an American TV programme which was popular in the 1950s, Andy being the "good sheriff". When pressures got too much, which happened frequently especially in the aftermath of the Gulf War, he would fetch some candy bars from the local shop (an extension to the El Sarras family home, our school neighbours) and we would watch an Andy Griffith video. Somehow that released the tension and we could laugh again. I introduced Brice to the English way of spelling and he made sure his friends and family back in Ohio knew he had an English secretary and that his spelling hadn't gone to pot.

Brice and Lydia had agreed to come to the School for a two year period and Brice's teaching job in the U.S.A. was kept open for him. The two years simply flew by and again it was time for me to say goodbye to another family who had become part of me.

It was hard but it wasn't the only farewell I had to make that June of 1992, I had to say farewell to George Shawrieh and all at the School because the Lord had shown both George and I that it was time for us to leave Hope School. How that came about I will share in a later chapter.

Chapter 8
Bethlehem Bible College

The video presentation of Bethlehem Bible College starts with the words – "BETHLEHEM, A CITY OF ROMANCE – HISTORY – AND BLESSING. Bethlehem was the setting for the Biblical romance between Ruth and Boaz. It was the birthplace of their grandson King David who tended his flocks on the hills nearby. It was here that he was inspired to write the 23rd Psalm. From the seed of David, Jesus the Messiah, was born in a manger and began his life among us..."

Bethlehem, the little town, which is in the thoughts of people all around the World each year at Christmastime. Its very name conjures up feelings of wonder, joy and awe. Thoughts that are concentrated on the events that happened 2,000 years ago when God sent His Son, born of a virgin, to be the Saviour of mankind. I doubt though, if there are many who wonder about the people who live in Bethlehem today and what their life is like. Yet the baby who was born in the manger grew up to manhood, was crucified, died and was buried BUT on the third day He rose again and ascended into heaven and is seated on the right hand of the most High, because:

> *"God so loved the World that He gave His only begotten Son that, whosoever believeth in Him should not perish but have everlasting life."*
>
> *John 3 verse 16.*

"Whosoever believeth in Him." On the day of Pentecost there were Arabians present who — "did hear them speak in their own tongue the works of God." Who heard and who believed. Today in Bethlehem there are Arabians, Palestinian Arabs, who have heard the "Good News" and have believed and accepted the Lord Jesus Christ as their personal Saviour. Bishara Awad, is one such believer, and it was whilst he was serving the Lord as Principal of Hope Secondary School that he was given the vision to establish a Bible College.

Bethlehem, along with the adjacent towns of Beit Sahur (Shepherds Fields) and Beit Jala is at the centre of the Palestinian Christian Community on the West Bank. Today's political unrest and conflict have made their mark on the communities in the area, bringing suspicion, hatred and discouragement. However, despite this there is still a star of love, peace and hope to be found at Bethlehem Bible College.

The College was founded in 1979 as an initiative of the local Arab Palestinian community in response to a shortage of trained workers for the local churches and Christian Institutions. It has indigenous leadership and is governed by a local board of trustees representing various denominations. It is a truly interdenominatial college and offers courses combining high academic standards with an encouragement to a deep spiritual commitment to Christ. Courses are offered in Biblical history, Content and Theology, Pastoral Ministry, Christian Education, Missions and Evangelism, Music and Counselling as well as general educational topics such as English and Biblical languages. It also offers a program for foreign students and new comers to the country interested in Christian service in the Middle East and teaching in the Arabic language.

It is, however, more than just an institution, it is a centre of peace, hope and reconciliation, a place where the light of Christ shines forth into a dark and troubled world.

Just before I arrived in July 1982, to work as Secretary at the College (which was then situated on the road from Manger Square to the Shepherds Fields) Alex Awad and the students of the College were engaged in a house to house visitation of the Beit Sahour area of Bethlehem. At one home they visited, Nawel a mother of six children was visiting her aunt. Nawel listened as Alex and the students shared about Jesus. She was in a state of tension after suffering severe pain in her back for many years, a pain which the doctors were unable to cure. The pain and her situation had brought her into a deep depression. After Alex and the students had finished sharing about Jesus, she said that she would like to know this Jesus they were talking about and would they pray for her back problem. They did and left the home. The next morning Nawel was waiting at the Bible College. She told them that the pain in her back had gone and that she had had the first good nights sleep in years. She then said she would like to enrol as a student at the Bible College. Consequently her whole family became believers. Nawal for many years helped to run a Sunday School programme in Beit Sahur and is a strong witness for the Lord.

Another student who was touched by the Lord through Bible College had been actively involved in the communist party. He had married and was looking for a job to support his new wife and approached Alex Awad to see if he could help. Alex was able to arrange a teaching position at Hope School for him and invited him to study at the Bible College. Bassam thought it was the least he could do to repay Alex's kindness and also he wanted to find out how "these Christians thought". After attending the college for a few months, listening as he says to the effective word of God, he one day walked home from the Bible College. He went straight to his room, shut the door and went down on his knees and asked the Lord to come into his heart. He is now involved in full time Christian work.

Other graduate students are serving God in their own communities in the Middle East, particularly on the West Bank and in Israel. These men and women work as teachers and church leaders. Some are pastoring churches, some are working in the caring professions and some have gone back to other careers where they are now more equipped to serve God and to witness for their faith. Some have gone on to study for advanced degrees.

Whilst I was working at the College, Bishara and Alex attended a Conference in Cyprus where they met with some Jewish believers. On their return they all began to meet together for prayer and fellowship. Out of these times grew the Arab/Israeli Believers Fellowship with Arab believers and Jewish believers meeting together on a monthly basis.

Not always an easy situation but a definite attempt to reach out to each other as brothers and sisters in Christ. With the coming of the Intefada the meetings became more difficult for many reasons and gradually became less frequent.

However a new initiative taken by Salim Munayer, a lecturer at the Bible College, has recently come to fruition. **MUSALAHA** — a ministry of Reconciliation. Salim's vision and belief is that our Saviour Jesus Christ not only reconciled humanity to God but also humanity to each other. Salim says that Ephesians 2 teaches us that Jesus broke through the natural barrier of race and culture which existed in His time and that His act on the cross is as relevant and true today as it was 2,000 years ago, especially in the land of His birth, death and resurrection. For this reason, Arab and Jewish leaders who believe in the Messiah have joined together with Salim's vision to create Musalaha. Musalaha is an Arabic word which means forgiveness and reconciliation between Palestinian Arabs and Jews in the Holy Land.

In January 1990 an application was submitted to the Ministry of Interior for recognition as a non-profit organisation. Approval of the application was received in December 1990. The activities Musalaha are sponsoring are:

(1) Seminars teaching from Scripture about reconciliation and the new commandment of our Lord — to love our enemies.

(2) Publishing material written in both Hebrew and Arabic, including personal stories of reconciliation.

(3) Cultural Teaching — attempting to promote understanding between the two dominant cultures which make up the peoples of the Holy Land.

Activities have been held bringing Arab Palestinians and Israeli Jews together to learn of each other's cultures, traditions and experiences. Musalaha seeks to promote a Biblical stance that both Arab and Jewish believers should take concerning the enmity between these two peoples. A stance that believes that only Christ can be a reconciler between humanity and God and between humanity and itself and that Christ is the only way.

Another initiative of the Bible College that began whilst I was working there was to invite visitors to Bethlehem on Christmas Eve into the College for refreshments and a programme of Christian music, drama and worship. Unfortunately this had to stop with the coming of the Intefada but I will share more about these special Christmas Eves in a later chapter because no book about Bethlehem would be complete if it didn't include a chapter on "Christmas in Bethlehem".

Carols and Christmas songs play a big part in Christmas celebrations all around the world. Singing and making a joyful noise unto the Lord are part of the Christian heritage and so it is no surprise that the Bible College has its own Choir. A Choir that has travelled from Nazareth in the North to Gaza in the South ministering in song and testimony as well as making two visits to England. It was hard for me to stay in Bethlehem knowing the Choir members would be singing in my home city of Bristol and meeting with my friends and family. But someone had to hold the fort in Bethlehem and it was so good to receive letters from home telling me how much the Choir members had blessed those who heard them sing and give their testimonies.

Other ministries undertaken by the College staff and students are Sunday School work, involvement with the Friendship Centre at Bethlehem University, and local nursery and day care. The College Library is open to the community and the College is frequently the meeting place for both local believers and a large number of visitors from all over the world.

A new, major ministry, is the Al-Aman Counselling Centre based at the College. This Centre seeks to positively enhance the emotional health, psychological well-being and spiritual stability of Palestinian individuals, families, schools and institutions. They are particularly concerned in areas of drug abuse, marital stresses and alcohol dependence.

In September 1990 the Bible College moved to a new

home on the Hebron Road. The Bible Lands Society of High Wycombe, England, very generously allowed the Bible College free use of the three buildings which were originally the Helen Keller Home and which had been standing empty for a number of years. I was with Bishara on the afternoon of 1st September 1990 (which also happened to be Bishara's birthday) when Peter Emerson of the Bible Lands Society handed over the keys of the buildings. I enjoyed greatly being the "official" photographer of the handing over ceremony. The first building we entered hadn't been used for over 22 years except by the "birds" who had found a safe nesting place. Even though everything was covered in a film of dust, the former grandeur of the building could be seen and it was exciting to realise its potential. At the opening ceremony in the spring of 1992 the transformation was incredible. The beautifully patterned tiled floors shone with new life and the big wooden doors covered previously in paint had been stripped to the original beauty of the mahogany wood. The Lord had provided and still is providing, capable and enthusiastic volunteers to renovate and remodel the new buildings. With the additional classroom space and dormitories the College hopes to be able to increase its enrolment and expand its ministry to which it has been called by God. With the buildings however, comes a financial challenge of raising adequate funds for their outright purchase by 1995.

In Bishara's personal testimony he says, "Returning to the West Bank I began to realise that only through trained spiritual leadership and the power of the Holy Spirit could the bitterness of the past be turned around. Over the years God has shown us His love and faithfulness as this dream has turned into reality". Bishara continues, "The College is prayerfully looking to its many friends all over the world to share with them their hopes and vision of a strong centre for academic and spiritual excellence and reconcilion in Bethlehem. A true 'radiating star' of hope, love and peace in the Middle East."

Chapter 9
His Lambs

One of the last jobs I did before leaving Bristol to go to Bethlehem was to pack into boxes my Sunday School materials and Pathfinder Teaching aids. I handed them over to Liz Brazier at St. Nathanael's Church to give them to whoever agreed to take over from me. In my mind I was thinking that Sunday School and Youth Work as such were things of the past for me. I suppose it was because of the language barrier, I could never see myself learning enough Arabic to teach a Bible Class.

However, once I was settled into the Church of God in Jerusalem and in Beit Jala where I lived, the door was opened for me to teach Sunday School. First I was asked if I would be willing to take a class on Sunday mornings during the English speaking service. That presented no problems, the lessons were in English and the age range from 2 to 10 years. That was something I was happy to do and from which I got lots of fun and enjoyment. I managed to get Sunday School syllabuses sent over from England and had no difficulty in adapting them. I remember especially the syllabus for January to April 1983. The theme was the re-building of the walls of Jerusalem by Nehemiah and the teachers notes said to make a model of the wall. "There is no need to do that", I thought to myself, "I will just take the children down the hill, over the Brook Kidron, up the other side and we can look at the real wall"! and that is just what we did. On Palm Sunday we read the account of Jesus's entry into Jerusalem and then walked down the Mt. of Olives to the Lion Gate where Jesus entered the city. In the afternoon we watched the present day procession of pilgrims carrying their palms and singing as they walked. Visual aids already provided! It seemed too good to be true. At Christmas time we would prepare a Christmas Programme to present to the Church. One year the programme included a Birthday

Lynn's natural parents. Rose and John Dixon on their wedding day, 28 July 1939.

Wedding Group with Daisy and James Weaver (Lynn's adoptive parents) on the far right.

Lynn at her adoptive parent's home in Shirebrook, Derbyshire.

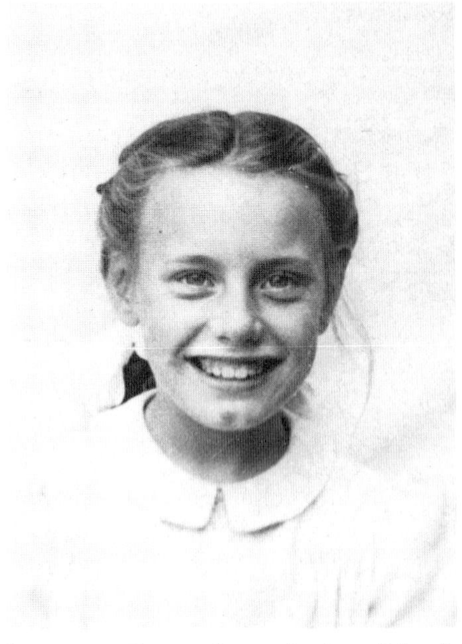

Lynn at Carter Lane Junior School, Shirebrook, Derbyshire.

Lynn with her adoptive parents, Daisy and James Weaver at their home in Bristol.

Lynn's Baptism in the River Jordan, Ju
1980.

Lynn at Pathfinder Camp, 1977.

ɔpe School – students and faculty 1984.

ɔpe School Faculty 1987. Principal Alex Awad, centre.

Hope School Faculty 1988. Principal Solomon Douhne, centre.

Hope School Faculty 1922 – in Chapel. Principals Brice and Lydia Brenneman holding their childre
Jonathon and Jameel.

ynn at her desk in Hope School.

ɜethlehem Bible College Students in the old premises. Bishara Awad translating for lecturer Duane Rogers.

The Douhne Family – Stephanie, Sue, David, Solomon, and Stephen.

The Hssen Family – Riet, Issam, Jonathon, Marianne-Lynn, Helene and Suzanna.

ngela Douhne.

The Awad Family 1985 – Alex, Randy, Christy, Brenda and Basem.

ľhe Kielwein Family (Church of God) – Martin ıolding Tobias, Jennifer, Vecky, Sascha and eanette.

The Brenneman Family – Lydia, Jameel, Jonathon and Brice.

Margaret, Lynn's 'Mother in Israel'.

The Schmidgall Family (Church of God) Amadeus, Gsbi, Yasmine, Paul and Sebastian.

Lynn in Arabic dress made by Imm Mustaffa whose home Lynn visited in the Refugee Camp.

Christy, Basem and Randy Awad 1990.

he Awad Family – Samir, Bishara (Principal Bethlehem Bible College) Dina, Salwa and Sami.

.ynn with the Nade Shabbat (her girls) – Church of God Beit Jala.

Picnic in Jerusalem with Ghada (far right) before she fell and hurt her knee.

Bishara Awad with Olafor Johannsson from Iceland at Hope School.

Claude Abu Dayyeh with girls from the Bada Shabat.

dies Meeting, Church of God, Beit Jula with visiting friend Pauline Illsley, far right.

he Ghanem Family – Imm Ibrahim, Ibrahim, Jabre, Suzanne and Issach. The family Lynn lived with
uring the Gulf War.

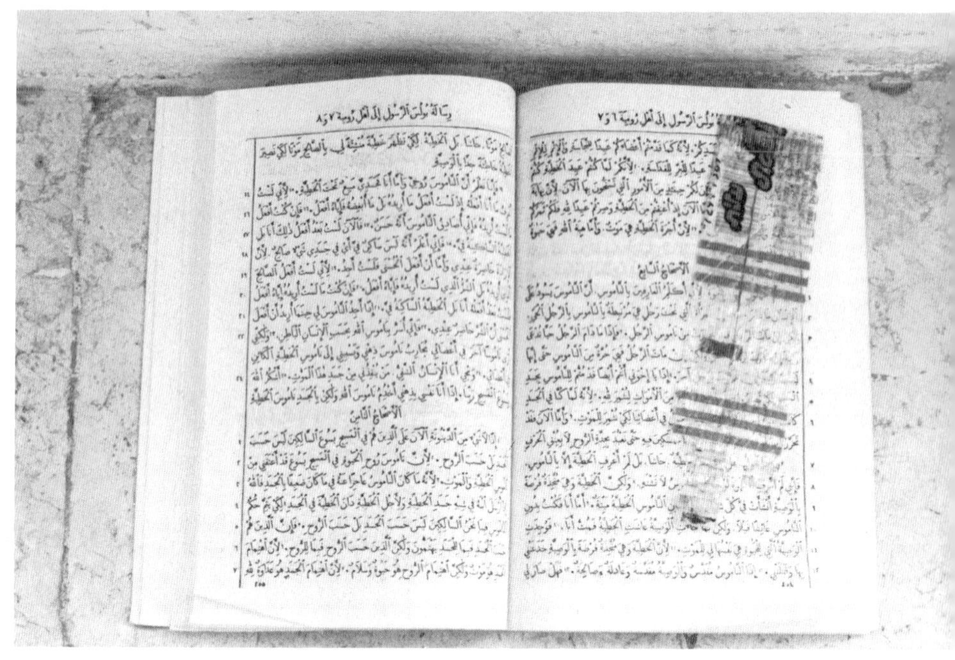

The Bible that Khader's mother sent him in prison and the chocolate wrapping paper the soldier ga Khader.

Lynn's room furnished with the help of Vecky Kielwein.

ynn with Imm Basem and the olivewood camels she and Abu Basem make.

ynn's sisters from left – Dorothy, Chris, Mary and Lynn. Taken at Niagara on the Lake 1987, one
onth before Dorrie's death.

Lynn on her 50th birthday, celebrated in Bristol with Juliette Durham (left) and Elsie Isaacs (right).

Lynn's apartment amidst the olive groves in Beit Jala.

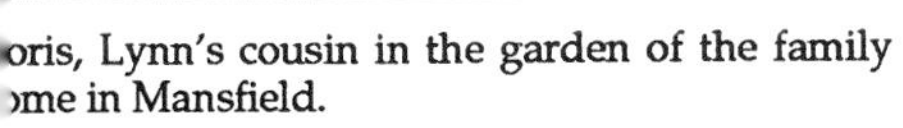

oris, Lynn's cousin in the garden of the family ome in Mansfield.

George Shawrieh, Secretary to Hope School.

ynn at the Church of God District Meeting at Aboud (Obediah's village).

Lynn with Ray, Liz and Helena Brazier and St Matthews Group in Jerusalem.

John and Janet Angle (bottom right) with Lynn (holding Jameel) and Palestinian Christians.

cake for Jesus, made in Bethlehem. On Easter Day we would go to the Garden Tomb for the Sunrise Service and have Easter breakfast together. The sights and smells of the Old City and being able to go to the actual places where Biblical events occurred made the Bible so much more alive for the children and they enjoyed it as much as I did.

Early in 1983, Gabi, the Church of God worker, was taken ill. She ran the Arabic Sunday School in Beit Jala which was held on a Friday afternoon as there was no School that day in order for the Moslems to respect their Holy Day. It was felt that it was best for her to return to Germany for medical treatment and before she left for Germany she visited with me and asked if I would be willing to teach her class of 11 to 15 year olds. Before I could respond she said, "You don't have to worry about the language, Imad and Nehad will translate for you". Very reluctantly I responded, "Alright but I will only be taking care of the class until you return from Germany. It's your class." So, very unsure of myself and rather nervously, with the help of Imad and Nihad (two Arabic young men who were brothers and who loved the Lord) I began to take the class.

I need not have been so nervous, these young people were precious and very soon became part of me.

In November of 1983, Martin the Pastor, came to visit me and asked if I would be willing to change the format of the class. I had been teaching boys and girls together and he felt that it would be better if this age group was split into a girl's group and a boy's group. He also felt it would be better if we changed the name from Sunday School and made it Youth Meeting. Teenagers are just the same the world over and Sunday School was a little too childish for them. So the Nadee Shabaat and Nadee Shabaab was born — Girl's Meeting and Boy's Meeting. I taught the girls with Nihad and Roni Shawrieh translating as Imad had left for the U.S.A. to study. Martin, and Atallah Esawi, who was now pastoring the Church of God in Beit Jala, would take the Boy's Meeting. We decided to include other activities like sports and crafts as well as the Bible Teaching because there was nothing much for the young people to be involved in other than those activities organised by the local Churches.

The new format involved a lot more preparation and time but it was worth it and it turned out that I wasn't given the chance to hand the class back to Gabi but it remained my concern until 1992. The reason that I didn't hand the class back to Gabi was that, although she returned to Jerusalem exactly one year after she had left, she did not return alone. She boarded the plane in Germany dressed in bridal clothes and on the arm of Paul Schmidgall, dressed as the English would say in "top hat and tails". They were met at Ben Gurion Airport by a reception committee and accompanied to the little Church of God on the Mt. of Olives for a special wedding ceremony at 9 p.m. in the evening followed by wedding cake and a real welcome back.

Everyone was so happy to have Gabi back, doubly happy because not only had she been healed by the Lord in spite of the doctors saying she would never work again, but the Lord had given her a husband. She did return to Sunday School in Beit Jala for a while but soon she was the mother of baby Sebastian and then another son, Amadeus. She and Paul then took over the pastorate of the Mt. of Olives Church of God as Martin and Veky Kielwein returned to Germany to oversee the Church of God Youth work, run a Youth Hostel and pastor a Church. To complete Gabi and Paul's family a little girl called Yasmeen was born to them in November 1989. So the Sunday School class I thought was to be in my care for a short while lengthened into 9 years. Not mine really, it was the Lord's and these were the lambs He wanted me to feed.

Sophie, Claude and Firass Abu Dayyeh, two sisters and their brother, were regular attenders when I first took over the class. These three young people, together with their parents George and Affaf (George is the English teacher at Hope School) became family to me and when Nihad left to go to the Church of God Bible College in Germany and Roni got a job in the Baptist Book Store in Jerusalem, Claude took over the translation for me.

Claude was a natural with teenagers and the girls came

to love her and week by week the numbers grew bigger and bigger until when they reached 40 girls we had to split the class. The younger girls met on Thursday afternoons and the older ones on Fridays. I never ceased to be amazed at their enthusiasms and even on winter days when the rain was heavy and everyone else was indoors they would turn up.

What did we get up to on those Thursday and Friday afternoons?... First we had a time of craft projects, then a refreshment break and ended with a devotional time, either a Bible study or a missionary story and always finished with a time of prayer. It was lovely to see the girls grow in the Lord.

We made several trips to Jerusalem, for in spite of living so close the girls didn't go there too often. They were not allowed to go without an adult and the political situation didn't make it easy for their parents to take them. The men have to have a permit from the army to be able to go to Jerusalem and sometimes the women also must have permission. Also most of the girls came from big families which meant brothers and sisters had to come along too. I never did come to terms with the fact that if we organised a picnic, or walk, or outing or party, younger brothers and sisters would turn up as well. Somehow there was always enough food to go around and room in the Church mini buses to squeeze in a few more.

Two separate trips to Jerusalem will always remain in my mind. On one occasion we took the girls to the Garden Tomb, General Gordan's site for Calvary. We entered the Garden and found seats in the shade of trees and then opened our Bibles to read the account of the first Good Friday evening and Easter Day —

> *"Now in the place where He was crucified there was a garden and in the garden a new sepulchre, wherein never man was yet laid. There laid they Jesus therefore because of the Jews preparation day, for the sepulchre was nigh at hand."*
>
> *John 19 verses 41 & 42*

> *"The first day of the week cometh Mary Magdalene early, when it was yet dark, unto the sepulchre and*

seeth the stone taken away from the sepulchre... and seeth two angels in white sitting, the one at the head and the other at the feet where the body of Jesus had lain... she turned herself back and saw Jesus standing and knew not that it was Jesus. Jesus saith unto her, 'Woman, why weepest thou? whom seekest thou?' She supposing Him to be the gardener, saith unto Him, 'Sir, if thou have borne Him hence, tell me where thou hast laid Him and I will take Him away.' Jesus saith unto her, 'Mary'. She turned herself and saith unto Him, 'Rabboni', which is to say, Master."

John 20 verses 1 to 16

After the Bible reading we walked around the Garden, to the platform overlooking the noisy Arab bus station but also looking across to the rock with the indentations like a skull —

"And He bearing His cross went forth into a place called the place of a skull which is called in Hebrew, Golgotha."

John 19 verse 17

We continued to walk through the Garden to look at the water cistern and wine press, finally we stood inside the empty tomb and read the notice on the door —

"He is risen, He is not here"

Luke 24 v 6.

Then before leaving the empty tomb we had a few moments of prayer and then filed out to let others come in. As we stood outside looking at the channel carved in the rock where the stone that sealed the tomb would have been rolled, Carol came up to me and she was shaking. Very concerned I said, "What is it Carol, what is wrong?" All she could reply was "It's Jesus, I know it's Jesus." Without a need for further explanation I knew that as Jesus had revealed Himself to Mary Magdalen on that first East Day so now He had somehow revealed Himself to a 14 year old Palestinian Arab girl. Time was to prove me right for after that she had a hunger and thirst for the things of the Lord.

In the second incident Jesus also revealed Himself but this time in a different way. Again Claude and I had taken a group of girls to Jerusalem. We had taken the bus to the top of the Mt. of Olives and walked down the mountain and into the Old City at Lions Gate or Stephens Gate as it is also known. It was through this gate that Stephen was taken and then stoned to death whilst Saul looked on (Acts Chapter 8). After looking in the shops in the Old City we came out at Damascus Gate, turned to the left where there is a grassy bank and sat for a picnic lunch. The sun was shining and the girls were in no hurry to move. They played chasing games, sang songs and enjoyed the freedom. Then one of the girls, Ghada (pronounced Raada) slipped and hurt her knee. She hobbled over to Claude and I, and sat on the wall for a while and then went back to join in the fun. A few moments later she let out a scream and collapsed on the grass. Going over to her I could see her knee was swelling like a balloon under her jeans. I had to think quickly what to do, so decided to send Claude to get a Service taxi (seven seater) to come to the spot and I would take Ghada and the girls who lived in Bethlehem with me in the taxi, Claude could then take the Beit Jala girls on the bus. The taxi came but would not park on our side of the road. He said we had to take Ghada across the very busy and wide road just below the Notre Dam Hotel. There we stood, Ghada in the middle with her arms around Claude and my shoulders and the other girls all excitedly milling around us. The traffic did not cease and the taxi driver kept calling us to step into the road saying the traffic would stop for us. Finally in blind faith we did step out into the oncoming traffic and it DID stop for us to cross. All the way to Bethlehem I was asking Jesus to touch the knee. We took the other girls home and finally arrived at Ghada's house. Only Ghada's mother was at home but she fetched her brother, Ghada's uncle, who took us to the Holy Land Christian Mission Hospital in Bethlehem. Ghada all this time was crying and couldn't put her foot to the ground. We helped her into the hospital and the receptionist sent for a doctor. He made Ghada try to walk unaided but she just cried out with pain. So he took her into a cubicle with her mother and uncle to examine the knee. I waited outside. As I waited Ghada's father came into the waiting room. He is a believer and we prayed together. Then he went with Ghada and her mother to the X-ray room. As they came back I noticed Ghada had stopped crying and although she was limping she was walking alone. We went into the cubicle to wait for the X-ray results and as we stood around the bed we visibly watched the swelling go down. When the X-rays came the doctor looked at them and said, "There is no damage whatsoever to the knee, you can take her home." A very different Ghada left the hospital, instead of tears there was laughter and I must say my heart was much lighter too. An added bonus was that because Ghada was under 14 and we had taken her straight to the hospital there was no charge made. Our Lord had taken care of every detail.

As well as Sunday School and the meetings for the 11 to 15 year olds, the Church of God in Beit Jala have a Shabeeba — Youth Meeting — for the 15 to 25 year old age range. Each summer the Shabeeba held a Youth Camp, usually sleeping at the Church on the Mt. of Olives. My girls class thought this was wonderful and kept asking, "Lynn, please may we have a camp?" Before saying yes, I decided to visit their parents to see if they would be willing to let their daughters sleep away from home. Both Arab Christian and Arab Muslim families guard their daughters carefully, especially when they enter their teens and most girls are married, usually by arrangement, by the time they are 18. Most of the parents, after I had promised that I would always be with the girls, even sleeping near to them, agreed to let the girls come but they were not so happy to let them sleep in Jerusalem. So we decided to have a camp at the Beit Jala Church of God for 3 days. For most of the girls it was the first time they had slept away from home and there was great excitement.

Each morning we would start with a Bible study. Then we had craft times, fun times of swimming and games, Christian films, trips, singing and ended the day with an epilogue. The first camp was so successful the girls almost immediately began asking for another one and their cry was

"Can we stay a week next time?" The following year we held another one of 5 days duration and the cry after this camp was "Can we stay a month next year?" I'm afraid that plea fell on deaf ears, it was a big responsibility caring for the girls away from their homes, but it was worth it all. Two incidents stand out as I look back on those happy times:

The second camp nearly didn't take place because of a water shortage. We were quite used to being without water in Beit Jala, sometimes for two weeks at a time. I usually managed because living alone I didn't use so much water and my tanks didn't completely empty before the next delivery came. The week before the camp, the water didn't come and I felt a little uneasy. The day before the camp I visited the Church and Pastor Attallah Esawi got in touch with the Water Company who assured him the water would come that night. It didn't so I contacted Attallah again — we had no telephone so I had to go to his house. He said he would go and buy water for us. Sixteen girls arrived after lunch, and we took them to Hope School for games. We arrived back at 5 o'clock to prepare the evening meal only to find there was still not one drop of water in the whole building. I sent Claude to tell Attallah and she returned to say he was not at home. "I'm sorry girls", I said, "If the water hasn't come by the time we have had supper, I will have to send you home." That was unthinkable to them but I knew I couldn't keep them without any water and if they had to go home I had to get them to the taxi station before it got dark. Supper was finished and the girls sat looking at me, so I suggested we go into the Church section for the Epilogue and then they would have to go home. We began the Epilogue with a time of prayer and specifically asked the Lord to help us with this problem and then I told the girls to open their Bibles. As they picked them up we heard a truck pull up outside the building and the girls let out a great shout and rushed to the window — it was the truck with the water! The driver came in and told us he had been driving all round Beit Jala looking for tents, having been told the water was needed for a camp. He thought we were in tents!! The water was duly pumped into the tanks and the driver taken on a tour of inspection of the camp. His parting shot was, "Well all I can say is this is more like an hotel than a camp." The girls relaxed visibly and got down to the serious business of enjoying themselves.

Yes, it was a big responsibility and a lot of hard work but the comments of one of the girls at the last camp we held put it all into perspective.

On the last evening of that last camp the girls were ready for bed and sitting on their mattresses and having a time of fellowship with Claude and myself. Claude suggested that we go round the room and say thank you to God for one thing He had given us at camp. When it came to Hannady's turn, a young girl from Bethlehem, she said, "Please can I say thank you for two things? I want to say thank you to God for sending Jesus to die for me and I want to say thank you to Him because He knows that I have no sisters, only six brothers and through this camp He has given me each one of you as a sister."

(After the Intefada began in 1987 we weren't able to hold anymore camps because of the situation. Strikes and curfews etc. made it too big a responsibility to have the girls sleep away from their homes.)

As I have already mentioned, Mother's Day on the West Bank, is always celebrated on the 21st of March. The girls were used to making cards and gifts at School to take home to their mothers but they decided they would like to do something a bit more special and asked if they could have a party for their mothers at the Church. So we began to make plans. They decided to save a shekel a week for a month to buy a gift, then on the morning of the party we all went into Bethlehem to buy the gifts. We returned to the Church and made cakes, picked flowers and prepared the tables. A programme had been planned. One girl read about the mothers in the Bible, another read a poem and they all sang some songs. We showed slides of the various activities the girls had been involved in. Then they gave their mothers the gifts, made the tea and served the refreshments. The mothers were overwhelmed and said that no one had ever done anything like that for them. I too was overwhelmed because, when the time came to give the gifts to the mothers, the girls gave me two packages as well. Over the years I continued to receive gifts on Mother's Day, not only from the girls but from neighbours children as well. The doorbell would ring and I would find one or two children standing on the doorstep with a bunch of flowers or a gift in their hands, come to wish me a happy Mother's Day. To me these gifts made the following Bible verse so very real:

> *"Sing, o barren woman, thou that didst not bear, break forth into singing and cry aloud, thou that didst not travail with child, for more are the children of the desolate than the children of the married wife, saith the Lord."*
>
> *Isaiah 54 verse 1*

Before I actually came to the Bethlehem area and as I asked for prayer and shared about the Scripture the Lord was giving me, nearly everyone took "Feed My lambs" meant I was to work with children. One day as we were sharing together Liz Brazier said to me, "You know lambs aren't necessarily children, they can be new believers young in their walk with the Lord that need spiritual food." Those words remained with me as I settled into life on the West Bank and I kept myself open to the Lord's leading in this direction.

One day, during my first few months in the land, I was having a time of fellowship over a cup of tea with Brenda Awad. Brenda shared with me something that had been on her heart for a while. She and another American lady were hungry for Christian fellowship and had discussed starting a Ladies meeting for expatriates in the area to get together for prayer, Bible study and fellowship. She wondered if I would be willing to help her get the meeting started. As I was hungry too I willingly said yes. We decided it would be better if we could have a room in the Church of God rather than meet in homes. Solomon Douhne who was then Pastoring the Church and Martin Kielwein the Overseer, agreed we could meet in the Church. At the first meeting it was suggested that some Arab ladies might like to join the meetings as well and so we agreed to invite them. With the passage of time the expatriate ladies returned to their homelands leaving Gabi Schmidgall and myself together with about six Arab ladies. The expatriate ladies had taken it in turn to lead the Bible Studies as well as inviting guest speakers. After the expatriate ladies had left it was time to prepare the programme for another year. I thought the Arab ladies would take a turn to lead the Bible studies. However after taking my turn I asked who would lead the next meeting and they all looked at me and said, "You. We want you to take the meetings except when we have a speaker." So these ladies too were His lambs that needed feeding.

We would meet every two weeks, have a cup of coffee or tea, then a short Bible study and end with a time of prayer. The Bible really came alive for these ladies from Greek Orthodox and Catholic backgrounds. However I noticed it was the prayer time that really had an impact on them and over the years they learnt to bring their requests to the Lord and expected Him to answer them and we did see many wonderful answers to prayer.

Every now and then we would receive boxes of used clothing from Europe and the U.S.A. and wondered how we could distribute them to the people who really needed them. On a visit from the U.S.A. to her family in the West Bank, Hudda Awad (the mother of Bishara and Alex) joined us at one of the meetings and she suggested we have a Bazaar to sell clothes at a modest price and also make new things as well. So that is what we decided to do and added homemade cakes to the sale as well. With the money raised we bought rice, sugar, oil and tea for needy families. From the sale point of view it was a huge success and we sold all there was to sell. Organisation wise it was a little chaotic and we never did quite get it right at the subsequent Bazaars we held but as the end result was to help those in need I guess we achieved our goal.

The Bazaars were held in December and we were able to take gifts of food to needy families in time for Christmas. We also were able to buy a personal gift, usually warm clothing, for the residents of the only home for the elderly in Beit Jala and one year we bought socks and underwear for severely handicapped children cared for by the Arab Society for the physically handicapped in Bethlehem.

Most years as we distributed the gifts in December we did so in heavy rain and gales because the winter had begun. I well remember the night in 1988 when we took the food packages to those in need. That year we made up 15 parcels of groceries. The evening was wild with heavy rains and as we say in England "not fit to send the dog out". But we went, two by two. I joined Affaf Abu Dayyeh to go to a one roomed house in a nearby Refugee camp. As we entered the room the smell of fresh baked bread hit our noses. It was tabla, large flat rounds of bread. The lady in her Palestinian embroidered dress, head covered with a white shawl, was so happy to see us. Her sick husband sat quietly in a corner and three lively children jumped up and down. The mother explained the bread was a treat as it was St. Nicholas's Eve and she had nothing else to give the children. She insisted we take two rounds of the hot bread and as we left I thought to myself we couldn't have chosen a better night, in spite of the rain, to take our gifts — St. Nicholas's Eve.

The ladies who came to the meetings looked forward to the time of fellowship and especially enjoyed it when we arranged to have our meeting at the Church of God in Jerusalem. Most of their time was spent in Beit Jala or in Bethlehem shopping, so an outing was a special occasion.

Several of the ladies expressed a desire to visit the Garden Tomb as they had never been there and so one Thursday we were taken by Pastor Attallah in the Church Minibus. An English guide showed us around and Attallah translated. The ladies were full of questions and as the guide brought the tour to a close we were standing in the empty tomb. He told the ladies that he knew Beit Jala, knew of the difficulties they were living under and the fear that each one had in their heart for their sons. A fear that dreaded their sons being taken or being shot and wounded by the soldiers. The guide then said he would like to pray for the ladies right there in the Tomb before they left. He closed the door and then in prayer asked the Lord to watch over and protect each family represented there. The ladies were visibly moved. As they came out into the sunshine they made their way to some seats and as they sat and reflected Attallah read from the Bible, in Arabic, the account of Jesus's burial and resurrection.

We returned to Beit Jala and I spent the rest of the afternoon working at Hope School. In the evening on my way home I decided to call in on Affaf Abu Dayyeh. I found her with Hynd who had also been with us to the Garden Tomb. The two of them had been talking about the visit and they reminded me of the two on the walk to Emmaus —

> *"And they talked together of all these things that had happened... and their eyes were opened and they knew Him."*
>
> *Luke 24 verse 13 to the end*

It was obvious that these Palestinian ladies had been touched by Jesus when they had visited the Garden Tomb.

His Lambs — Palestinian teenage girls and Palestinian mothers — and He had chosen me to go and feed them. What an awesome task He had given me but He also promised me that —

> *"Everyone who has left house, or brothers, or sisters, or father or mother, or wife, or children, or lands for MY NAMES SAKE, shall receive a hundredfold and shall possess life EVERLASTING."*
>
> *Matthew 19 v 29*

He has kept, and is still keeping that promise, abundantly...

Chapter 10
Whoever Gives Up... Shall Receive...

Tour groups were a regular feature at Hope School and the Bible College and all blessed us in so many ways. Support for the ministries and new friendships for me personally, blossomed with each group that visited.

Shortly after I arrived, and at the end of one such visit from a group from the U.S.A., a lady walked up to me and said, "I have a word from the Lord for you." My startled look could not have put her off because she continued with the words, "Thou shalt dwell in the land in safety and I shall make fat thy bones!" The safety bit sounded alright but I wasn't so sure about my bones being made fat. I was a petite English size 12 at the time and was quite happy to remain so. Though I certainly wasn't plump enough for my Palestinian friends! Returning to Brenda and Alex Awad's home the next afternoon I found a delicious chocolate cake sitting on the kitchen table. "Where did that come from", I asked Brenda. "I baked it", she replied and with a twinkle in her eye she said, "I thought I had better help make the prophecy come true"!

The coming years were to show me that the Lord did use people to fulfil that word to me, not only to provide me with food and drink but with clothes, furniture, finances, books, cassettes and even flowers. I did indeed dwell in the Land in safety though I did experience some hair raising situations.

"My God supplied all my needs" (Philippians 4 v 19).

As I have already shared, the first major provision the Lord made for me was my apartment in the Church of God in Beit Jala. When I moved in, I had a bed to sleep on, a chair to sit on, a table to eat from, a cupboard with drawer space for my clothes, shelves on the wall for my books, curtains at the window and a rug on the floor. The kitchen had a cooker, a fridge and crockery belonging to the Church but which I was free to use. I looked with satisfaction around my new home and thought I have all I need. I was content.

One afternoon after I had been in the apartment about a year, Veky Kielwein, from the Church of God on the Mt. of Olives, came to visit me. She stood in the doorway of my room and let her gaze wander over the room, then she said, "If you are going to stay here we have to do something with this room, have you any money to buy furniture?" Veky is a born home-maker and I came to recognise that "gaze" over the next few weeks as she transformed the room. My reply to Veky was, "Well I have been thinking about getting a new bed, this one is narrow and creaks everytime I turn over, but I don't know if I can afford to buy any more furniture, leave it with me for a few days."

That evening I asked the Lord if it was alright for me to buy some new furniture. The next lunch time the mail arrived at Hope School and I received a letter from my sister Dorothy, in Bristol. Her opening remarks were, "I have just returned from your Bank to deposit a cheque for £375 for you, it is an Income Tax rebate. I thought you would like to know"!

I called Veky to tell her the news. A few days later I heard someone come into the Church and went to see who it was and found Martin, Veky's husband, together with Bent, a Danish young man, armed with stepladders, paint and brushes. They had come to paint my room. They left a message to say Veky would fetch me the next day to go and buy furniture. She took me to a shop in Bethlehem that sold cane furniture and we chose a bed, bedside table, a large bookshelf, a lounge chair and a desk. When it came to pay she grabbed my purse from my hand and said, "Go for a walk, I want the shop owner to think the furniture is for me, she knows me, and if she thinks it is for you she will charge more!" So as I left the shop I could hear Veky bargaining away. Finally she came out of the shop with a big grin on her face, satisfied she had obtained a good price. The furniture was loaded into the minibus and we drove it back to the apartment. Martin and Bent unloaded it and Veky and I arranged the room. When things were in place we realised we didn't have a chair for the desk. "Never mind", I said, "I'll use a chair from the Church". As it was a Friday afternoon I then left Veky as I had to take the Girl's meeting. After the meeting I went back into my room and found a lovely cane chair sitting neatly in place under the desk. Veky had gone out and bought it.

Over the next few weeks she appeared with new curtains, a lovely light fitting, a table lamp, pictures for the walls and ornaments for the shelves. Finally she stood one more time and "gazed" around the room. "Veky", I remonstrated, "the room is perfect it doesn't need any more." "There needs to be something on that wall", she said, "I think a Bedouin donkey rug would look just right there. Next time I go to Bir Sheva market I'll get you one," and she did!

Over and over again the Lord's words, "I will stablish, strengthen, settle you", came back to me.

At first I ate my mid-day meal at the School or College and had my breakfast and evening meal in my apartment but as the village people began to get to know me, my evening meal was very often shared with them in their homes. The Palestinians are the most hospitable people I have ever known, you cannot even knock on the door of their homes without usually being given something — a drink, a piece of fruit or chocolate. Sometimes I became overwhelmed with their kindness and generosity. Even walking home from School the ladies would invite me into their homes and proceed to give me bread they had baked that day, or a bag of fruit that was in season. Sometimes it was hilarious, especially when the apricots were in season. I remember a week in 1989 when I had a friend from the U.S.A. staying with me. Ruth Val-Jean Fox was painting a mural in the School Chapel and lived with me whilst she was working on it but more about that later. Each evening of that week in June as I came home I deposited a jar of apricot (mish-mish in Arabic) jam on the kitchen table. On the Saturday as I walked into the kitchen, Val looked at what I was holding in my hand and said, "Oh no, not another jar of apricot jam!" It was! I can think of nothing nicer than sitting with a round of freshly baked bread, tearing off a piece and dipping it into a dish of fresh apricot jam and popping it into my mouth. I for one was quite happy that Beit Jala was famed for its mish-mish trees.

Imm Mustafa, one of the ladies who cleaned at the School, would bring me bread and little pasties with spinach inside as well as toot, (mulberries), figs and grapes. She lives in the Dehaisha Refugee Camp with her family and although she spoke no English and my Arabic is limited, we grew to love one another very much. She kept asking me to visit her home and I finally agreed, in spite of my neighbours telling me it wasn't safe to go alone to the Refugee Camp. "I'm not going alone, I'm going with Imm Mustafa", was my response and one day after school I walked along the road with her to get the bus to her home.

It was my first visit to a Refugee Camp and as we entered I noticed the open sewers running down the narrow lanes between the small houses. Houses with just two rooms for the families who lived in them. Families who had all been turned out of their own houses in the villages in 1948 and who were still living in these dwelling places provided by the United Nations.

When I arrived at Imm Mustafa's house I was pleasantly surprised. It was at the end of a row and so had more space and even a little garden with a grape vine and flowers. Her second son Mohammad, was home and one of her daughters, they both spoke good English and Mohammad's friend who joined us later also spoke good English, so I was able to relax and enjoy the visit.

I was served in the normal Arabic way. First with a glass of juice, then a bowl of fruits was brought in and I was served a plate which had grapes, apples and bananas on it. In time I had come to learn I didn't have to eat all I was given and to my relief, I found it was quite acceptable if I just ate only one piece of fruit. Finally I was served the black Arabic coffee, after which it is in order to leave, the visit being over. So on this occasion, after the coffee, I rose to leave but was immediately told to sit as supper was being prepared for me. What a supper — a tray piled high with rice and chicken, soup from the chicken with potatoes and parsley in it, olives, bread, salad plus a glass of goat's yogurt to drink. That was something I had to decline, the sharp, acrid taste as it hit the back of my throat and the smell made tears come to my eyes. The rest of the meal I was able to enjoy and after eating my fill and then being given a towel to wipe my hands on (most of the meal was eaten with my fingers) I felt this time I could rise and take my leave.

Mohammad and his friend said they would escort me to the main road to get a taxi and as I came out of the room in to the yard Imm Mustafa came from her kitchen with a bag of fresh bread for me. She then proceeded to cut a huge bunch of grapes from the vine and pick a bouquet of flowers from the small garden and place them all in my arms. I turned to her daughter and said, "Why is she giving me all this?" The daughter looked at me surprised and replied, "My mother loves you."

The young men walked with me through the camp squalor to the main gate. Mohammad hailed a taxi, his friend opened the door for me to get in and then Mohammad said, "I have told the taxi to take you to your home and I have paid him the fare". As the taxi drew away tears flowed down my cheeks. Here was I, my arms full of bread, fruit and flowers, my heart full of the love bestowed on me by this Moslem family and there stood these two young men, smiling and waving goodbye before turning to return to their home. A home in a Refugee Camp, surrounded by barbed wire (later the wire was replaced by corrugated tin panels) and a home that was constantly put under curfew meant the family had to stay inside the two rooms sometimes for weeks at a time, with no electricity or water and until the curfew was lifted, only being allowed out for a few hours occasionally to buy food. A home that would later bear bullet holes from soldiers shooting into the house and narrowly missing Mohammad's baby daughter.

For Mohammad later married and I was present at the wedding celebrations when he brought his bride to his home and the baby daughter who escaped the soldier's bullets had a name very similar to mine. She is Rosleen and I am RosaLINd. This family was used by the Lord to bless me abundantly!

During my first year in Bethlehem, if I heard of a tour group coming I would write and ask them to bring things from England that I couldn't get locally or if I could get them, they were very expensive. Everyone was good and brought the things I asked for and always when I took out my cheque book to pay for the things, I would meet with the same response – "These are a gift from us". A pattern seemed to be emerging with the gifts and I began to realise the Lord was teaching me a lesson. If I asked, say for a jar of coffee, I would get two from different sources. Many people would bring me things that I hadn't asked for but which I really did need and when I asked them why they had brought them they usually replied, "We thought they might be useful". One friend, Peggy Lazar from Texas, told me she would go into the store, stand at the entrance and say, "Lord, You know what Lynn needs, guide me to get the right items." So my joy when I opened her packages to find warm winter pillowslips, a pair of cosy shoe linings (just what I needed for my boots) and little luxuries like bath oil, perfume, or a new nightie or slippers, just thrilled me.

Slowly it dawned, the Lord knew what I needed, there was no need for me to ask.

Life became exciting and breathtaking as He provided. Someone would bring a skirt, someone else a sweater or blouse and they would match. My wardrobe has taken on a whole new meaning. Any day as I dress I can think with affection of the sisters and brothers in the Lord who have given me the items of clothing I am putting on. I have shoes, slippers, sweaters, blouses and underwear all supplied by friends and family in England, Canada, U.S.A., Sweden, Germany, Jerusalem and Beit Jala. Imm Jacob (the mother of Sawsan Ghawali a teacher at Hope School) is a prolific knitter. She uses no patterns and makes up her own designs and each year she knits for her husband, three sons, two daughters, two grandchildren and me. Why me? Simply because Sawsan is my friend and sister. So now I am the proud owner of hand knitted, designer made sweaters in pink, rose, blue, white and lavender.

I also receive financial support, books, cassettes and even the English Women's Weekly magazine from friends around the world. All arrive just when needed the most.

So many times tears of gratefulness for the goodness of the Lord have flowed and I decided that each day I would record in my diary the love gifts I received. The list makes interesting reading: Fruit/flowers/soap/tea-pot/books/cassettes/cheques and money/cotton gowns from Jordan/Earl Grey Tea/Cushion covers/ corn on the Cob/jewellery/pictures/almonds/pomegranates/ grapes/craft materials/ olive oil/dress material/tooth paste/ shampoo/jam/table clothes/tea towels/ peanuts/ bread/crystallised apricots/vinegar/ dates/fish/etc. etc...

The love gifts are not only material but meet needs in all areas of my life. So many times when I have needed transport a taxi driver or friend would pull up as I walked out of the door and take me to where I wanted to go.

When I needed an expression of human love the Lord would meet that need, often through the hugs of little ones and when I needed companionship He would send friends to visit me or to live with me for a period of time. He gave me a friend and mother in Jerusalem, I spent many weekends in fellowship with Margaret.

One special way He has met my needs is in His provision of new friends around the world who uphold me in prayer and support. In my homeland of England, he has brought into being, Friends of Hope School, (a Trust that has recently been renamed Hope Christian Trust). The Trustees, besides myself are Ray and Elizabeth Brazier, my vicar and his wife, and John and Janet Angle. The Lord brought John and Janet into my life one snowy New Years day in January 1983 when they visited the College and School after being told about them by friends. He has laid a love on their hearts for me personally and for the Palestinian people. He has used them to bless me abundantly and to bless all at Hope School, Bethlehem Bible College, House of Hope for the Blind and many individuals in the Bethlehem area. Although they live in Clevedon, which is just a few miles from my family home in Bristol, they had to come to Bethlehem that cold snowy day to meet me... truly our friendship is from the Lord.

The blessings showered on me have overflowed to the School, the College, the Church and my friends and neighbours in Beit Jala. Tour groups visiting brought many gifts for the students. Footballs/basket balls/sweaters/notebooks/pens/pencils/and table games. One friend sent a new set of typing books for the typing class. Two of the students, Juanna and Nadia Billeh were provided for in a special way. The girls suffer from a blood disease, Thalassaemia Major, which means they have too much iron in their blood and they have to have regular blood changes. Treatment is vital to prolong their life span. Medicine and hospital treatment are very expensive and the family have no father to support them. Fortunately they have Insurance to pay for their hospital treatment. However modern science has developed a pump which can be fitted to patients and thus prevent the frequent blood transfusions and also extend life expectancy. The cost of one pump is about $700 and no way could the family of Juanna and Nadia find the money. We shared the problem with friends of Hope School in England and Elizabeth Brazier (the Secretary) shared it with other Christians in the Bristol area, especially with Sandra Lawrance from Nailsea. Sandra prayed about the situation and began to share the need. Gifts of money came pouring in and Dr John Gilmore, a Nailsea doctor, was able to bring the pumps from England together with medicine.

The Bible College benefited with many new books for the College Library and volunteers to renovate the new buildings.

Trinity Tabernacle, a Church in Bristol, sent a suitcase of lovely, brand new dolls, which we gave to the girls in the Sunday School one Christmas.

Groups brought clothes and shoes which I shared with neighbours. Theresa Southern, another friend from Bristol, but who like John and Janet, had to come to Bethlehem to meet me, filled her suitcases with craft material and came for three weeks to teach the girls and ladies new crafts.

One wonderful way the Lord provided was in the transformation of the Hope School Chapel. Ever since I arrived at the School it had been my desire to make the Chapel nice. I felt shame when I took visitors into it for the chairs were broken, there was old brown pews, chipped paint and torn hymn books. This was the room where we began each day with the Lord and yet it was the worst room in the whole School. Somehow there was never enough money to buy paint and new chairs. Week by week we told the Lord we wanted to make the Chapel nice.

Then one day in 1988 we received a letter from Myra and Allan Page saying their Methodist Church in Llanyafron, Cwmbran, Wales, had decided to make Hope School their Mission Project for 1988/89. So we decided to use the money raised for the Chapel. My desire was to have the walls re-painted, and to buy new chairs and curtains but what does the Lord say.

"My ways are not your ways..."

Isaiah 55...

His way was to send us Ruth Val-Jean Fox, an interior designer and artist from North Carolina, who stayed with me from May to September 1989. During that time she painted a mural on the Chapel facing wall, of the Lord Jesus surrounded by children, animals, flowers, trees and water. On each beam across the Chapel she painted Scriptures with illustrations in English and Arabic, with the help of a sign writer from Bethlehem. On the back wall she painted John 3 v 16 *"God so loved the World that He gave..."* The walls became a deep pink with a border of turquoise and red and the old brown pews were painted the same colours. Carpet was laid on the floor and new chairs and hymn books were purchased. The Chapel had become not only a place to meet daily with the Lord, it had become an oasis of blessing and peace.

I truthfully could write a whole book on the subject of God's provision but I trust this chapter has shown a glimpse that :

"He who promised is faithful" — Hebrews 10 v 23.

My heart overflows with gratefulness as I see day by day how He does provide. I also react to His provision with awe as I look back and see not only His provision of necessities but His provision of the little things that bless. I love flowers and can rejoice even at a field of daisies and buttercups. In His love the Lord has provided me with an abundance of flowers in Bethlehem. Roses are a particular favourite and our garden in Belmont Road, Bristol was full of them. Somehow I thought I was going to miss going out into the garden and picking a few for my room but on my arrival at Hope School I found at least five flower beds planted with rose trees — yellow ones, pink ones, white ones, mauve ones and deep velvety red ones with a beautiful perfume. Sometimes I would pick them myself. Most times, Hanna Khoury the house-father, would walk through my office door with a big bunch in his hands for me. I also thought I would miss the English spring flowers but the Holy Land spring flowers grow in abundance around the School and my apartment — wild cyclamen, oxe eye daisies, miniature iris and red anemones. It became embarrassing in the Spring as neighbouring children rang my door bell bringing me armsfull. It thrilled me to see freesia and arum lilies growing in the gardens but there was one special bunch that surpassed them all...

In March, 1990, Rhondda Leadbeater (now Thomson) the Secretary of Hope Evangelistic Outreach in Toronto who sponsored the School came to stay with us for a month. She lived with me in my apartment and helped in the School. A few days before she returned to Toronto she gave me a farewell gift, a beautiful cut glass vase. I sat it on my desk in the evening and as I admired it, I thought to myself, "It's beautiful but a vase needs flowers. I'll have to wait though until I go to Jerusalem to buy some." It was a tall vase, too tall for the wild flowers and the roses at Hope School were not yet in bloom. The next day Rhondda and I worked late at the School and returned to the apartment early evening. As we walked up the steps I stopped and gasped for there hanging on the door handle was a huge bouquet of mixed garden flowers tied with a bow. I found out the next day that one of the girls from the Youth meeting had come to visit me and finding me not home had hung the flowers on the door...

Yes, the Lord does use people to bless us but I have come to learn that all the love-gifts originate from His prompting.

Now to the first part of that "Word from the Lord" I received back in 1982...

Chapter 11

Thou Shalt Dwell In The Land In Safety

To dwell means to live in a specified place, secure. The Lord had allowed me to dwell in the Bethlehem area, the place He had brought me to, by providing me with a Work Permit and Visa for the past ten years. They were issued on a yearly basis and were not always easy to obtain but always they came to ensure I could stay in the land legally.

When I first arrived and heard my Palestinian neighbours saying "they were working on their papers", I thought that was a strange expression but I came to experience at first hand what that means. You most certainly have to work hard to get any kind of paper to travel or remain in the Land. I missed whole days from the office at School and College waiting in line at the army headquarters — everything in the West Bank has to have the approval of the Military Governor before you can go to the Civil Offices. One time I went seventeen times to get a signature and a stamp on an application. Other times I would be given a visa for one month which expired the day after I got it and then I had to run from office to office to get a new application in or pay double fees. I was fortunate as I only had to go to three places to process my papers:

1. To the translator to get my application translated into Hebrew.

2. To the Military Governor's Office to get the application signed.

3. To the Civil Office and then wait a month before the papers were processed.

My Palestinian friends at one time had to go to five different offices to obtain signatures before going to the three I had to go to.

Yes I did have to work on my papers but it did mean I was able to dwell in the Land, the majority of the time in safety, but there were a few narrow escapes.

One escape happened not long after I started work at Hope School. The School on this occasion had been closed by Military Order and so there were no students or staff on the premises except Zuhair. He was an older student who helped look after the chickens. One Friday after the Youth meeting, I planned to go back with Veky Kielwein to spend the weekend in Jerusalem. Veky asked if we could first go up to the chicken farm at the School to buy eggs. As we approached the entrance to the farm we noticed the big double gates were closed. So I jumped out to open them and let Veky drive the mini bus through. As I pushed one side of the gate open I realised something was wrong and thought the gate had come off its hinges but couldn't understand why it was pushing me forward. The next thing I knew I was lying on the ground with the gate on top of me. What I didn't know, but Veky did because she saw the whole thing happening and was powerless to do anything, was that a huge block of concrete wall came down with the gate missing my head by a fraction. We learned later that earlier in the day a lorry had hit the wall and knocked a block off the wall and the drivers had just put it back in place without securing it.

Zuhair heard the crash of the gate coming down and came running out of the chicken farm. he was a strong young man and was able to lift the gate off me and help me up. I didn't appear to have any serious injuries but by the time we got to Jerusalem my arm was a beautiful shade of black and blue.

When I returned to School on Monday, I walked over to see the gate and wall myself and as I looked at the huge concrete block lying there on the ground, I shivered and sent up a prayer of thankfulness that all I had sustained from the incident was a badly bruised arm.

It seems strange that my next escape also involved Veky and the Church of God mini bus. On the morning of Tuesday, 15 July, 1985, the verse on the calendar hanging in my kitchen read —

> *"And it shall come to pass, that before they call, I will answer"*
>
> *Isaiah 65 verse 24*

As I read it, I said, "Thank you Lord for that promise". Little realising that before the day ended these words would come vividly back to mind and that my heart would be full of a greater thanksgiving to the Lord. It was a special day for me because two very dear friends, Roy and Sandra Lawrence, were coming to visit me from England and I was looking forward to having news from home and anticipating a sweet time of fellowship with them. So at 10 p.m. that evening I climbed into the mini bus with Veky and set off for the airport.

As we approached the highway from Jerusalem to Tel Aviv we saw two Israeli soldiers standing at the side of the road waiting for someone to stop and give them a ride. Veky slowed the minibus and turning to me said, "I don't usually stop but do you mind if we give the soldiers a lift, they are probably going home?" My immediate response was to say, "Yes, of course we would give them a lift." The soldiers were happy to get in and off we went down the highway heading for Ben Gurion airport.

A few kilometres further on we passed under a bridge crossing the road and the next few seconds became like a nightmare. From the bridge someone threw a huge stone right in front of the mini bus. It missed the wind screen by a fraction of an inch but went under the wheels and the mini bus went out of control. We realised later that there were many more large stones on the road which had also been thrown from the bridge. Veky steered the mini bus to the side of the road, though she said later that she wasn't aware of what she was doing, and we came to a halt.

One of the soldiers very calmly told us not to be afraid, all was well. Then the two of them ran back and cleared the stones to prevent further accidents. When they returned the one who had spoken before, looked at Veky and said, "God loves you, the accident could have been much worse." Both soldiers then proceeded to change the wheel which was crushed and in no time we were on our way again. The soldier who had done the talking, again reassured Veky, not to be afraid and told her that her driving was excellent. His calming tone was like a balm to our beating hearts and shaking limbs. Just before we reached the exit for the airport the soldiers asked to be let out and disappeared into the darkness of the night. We continued our journey just praising the Lord. As we reached the airport my friends had just come through customs and so our arrival time was perfect.

The next morning, Martin the Pastor and his brother Andreas, checked the minibus to find that there was damage to the undercarriage which needed to be welded in order to make the bus safe for future use.

We do not know why on this particular journey we were led to pick up the soldiers, we do not know who it was who threw the stones from the bridge but we do know that God kept His promise and answered us before we called upon Him and we praised His Name.

Several times I arrived back in Beit Jala from a visit to Jerusalem and would switch on my radio to hear that there had been a bomb attack, a shooting incident or stabbing in the area I had just been in and I would thank God for His protection.

On another occasion, again in the Church of God mini bus, but this time with the Beit Jala Pastor Attallah Esawi and his wife Hilda, we narrowly missed being stoned.

It was a Sunday morning and we were going to Church on the Mt. of Olives. We had heard on the radio that a Palestinian had stabbed three people in Jerusalem but the news didn't say where and so we decided to try and go. There were no road blocks and we continued to drive out of Bethlehem and into the suburb of Talpiot. We noticed lots of vans with police getting out of them and as we pulled up at a red traffic light we saw to our left, coming up a side street an angry shouting mob of young men. They suddenly began pointing to our van and began to cross the dual carriage way towards us when the lights turned green and Attallah sped away from them. They had spotted the blue number plate of the minibus, which meant we were Palestinians from the West Bank and in their anger at the stabbings, had come to take revenge on Palestinians coming into Jerusalem.

We were able to turn in to old Bethlehem Road and return safely to Beit Jala. We heard on the evening news that other "blue number plate" drivers behind us hadn't got away so easily and the windows and windscreens of their cars had been smashed to pieces.

Truly, the words from the lady in that tour group way back in 1982, came to pass for I did indeed, "Dwell in the Land in safety" and yes, my bones did become fat!! I am no longer a petite size 12 having gone up two more sizes on the scale but I can look on that now also as a love gift from the Lord. Why? Because it means my Palestinian neighbours have taken me to their hearts and show their love for me by the hospitality they bestow upon me. In their eyes to be on the plump side is beautiful and they really want me to be "one of them". At least, that is the way I look at it!

Chapter 12
A Piece Of Chocolate

Tears of sorrow and of joy play a role in most people's lives, they are a part of our shared humanity. We also experience times when tears won't come, when we become frozen, going about our daily lives mechanically because circumstances have overtaken us. In such times we can only say, along with Mother Basilea Schlink — "God I don't understand You, but I trust You."

One such circumstance overtook my close neighbours, myself, all at Hope School, Bethlehem Bible College and the Church of God. It lasted for 52 days in 1989 but the lesson it taught us all will last forever. **We can indeed trust God in all circumstance.**

In a way it involved only one person, a young man named Khader, whose name translated from Arabic to English is George. Most Christian families in the Bethlehem, Beit Sahour, Beit Jala triangle have a son called George, for the simple reason that St. George is the patron saint of the area. However it was the Lord Jesus Christ Himself who was watching over "our" Khader throughout those 52 days when indescribable things happened to him.

Khader graduated from Hope School, with good marks, decided that he would like to continue his studies at Bethlehem Bible College and enrolled as a student. In the February 1989 edition of the Bethlehem Bible College Newsletter, Bishara Awad the President included the following paragraph:

> *"We want to ask you to pray for one of our students. Khader was picked up after midnight on February 5, 1989 by the Israeli secret police forces from his home town in Beit Jala. Khader is a Christian and loves the Lord. We are not aware of him being involved in any political activities. No one is allowed to see him, not even his relatives or his lawyer. It is our prayer that*

he will be released soon. The Church in Bethlehem is praying for him, please join us."

Seventeen days after Khader had been dragged from his bed in the middle of the night, his parents went to ask if they could see him. They were told that he was still in solitary confinement as he hadn't confessed anything and therefore they were not allowed to visit. They were also told that a lawyer would be allowed to visit him and so his parents asked Bishara at the College and Solomon at the School if they could obtain a lawyer. His mother also asked if a lawyer could take Khader's Bible and some clean underclothes when he went to visit him.

This was arranged but it wasn't until Khader was released 35 days later that we heard what happened to him, his Bible and clothes after the lawyer left. Khader spent a total of 52 days in solitary confinement in a cell not big enough for him to stand up in, going many days without food and drink, not even being able to wash himself and undergoing torture.

Khader told us that after the lawyer departed, the soldiers standing around him grabbed the Bible and clothes, pushed him back into the cell and told him that when he confessed he could have them back. He said he sat on the bed and cried. Later that night he heard a knock on the cell door and a voice quietly calling him to the window. He went and saw a soldier standing there holding the Bible in his hand. The soldier said, "Is this your Bible?" Khader replied, "Yes". The soldier said, "Are you a believer?" Khader replied, "Yes". The soldier said, "So am I, take your Bible and hide it."

Khader said he held the Bible close to his chest and wept. Sitting there he wondered why the soldier had given him the Bible and he wasn't sure if he could trust him.

The soldier returned to the cell on other occasions, one time bringing a cheese sandwich but Khader's response to this was to say, "How do I know you haven't poisoned it?" The soldier's quiet reply was "Look at me" and he took a bite out of the sandwich. Another time the soldier brought a bottle of water and again Khader questioned if it was safe to drink, again came the quiet response "Look at me Khader" and then the soldier proceeded to take a drink. Khader said he drank the water and thought to himself "How can I know for sure that I can trust him". He had a very nasty taste in his mouth and was longing for a piece of chocolate and there in the cell he prayed this simple prayer. "God, if that soldier really wants to help me, let him bring me a piece of Elite chocolate". (Elite is Israeli made and the kind of chocolate Khader liked.) A little while later there came the knocking on the door that Khader had become used to and there once again stood the soldier. "I am very sorry, Khader," the soldier said, "I couldn't get you any bread but we have to keep your strength up, eat this," and he gave Khader a piece of Elite chocolate.

Khader said something happened to him and in that moment his desire to serve the Lord was born.

Easter for the Protestants and Catholics, came early that year. The Greek Orthodox celebrate Easter a little later.

That Easter of 1989, I was going to visit Martin and Veky Kielwein in Germany and so I left on 16th March returning to Beit Jala on March 27th, the day after Easter Day. Arabic custom is that if you have been away, then on your return, neighbours and friends must come to say "Hamdila As Salami" to welcome you back. I put my suitcase in my room and being British headed for the kitchen to put the kettle on for a nice cup of tea after the journey. As I did so my door bell rang and I found Khader's parents on the doorstep to welcome me home. They came in and sat together on my couch and shared the tea with me. As I looked across at them they looked so dejected that I was almost afraid to ask news of Khader. I was very relieved to hear his mother say, "We went to see Khader today Lynn." My heart leapt, "You saw him, how is he?" His mother looked at me, "No, Lynn we didn't see him, he is still in solitary confinement" and the tears slowly rolled down her cheeks.

The next morning I returned to School and began work on the mail piled high on my desk. At about 9.30 a.m. I heard the telephone ringing in the main office and then shouts all through the School — "Khader has been released". Solomon and some of the teachers immediately went to the house to welcome him back. I said I would go later when I had finished my work. Really I was afraid that I could not handle seeing him straight from prison and when I learnt that I would not recognise Khader, I knew that I couldn't handle it at that time. For not only had he not washed for 52 days, his beard had been plucked out, his head gashed open where it had been banged against the wall and he could not stand straight due to injuries inflicted on him.

His home was full of neighbours and friends come to welcome him back but it was not until the 2nd of April, six days after his release and when the house was empty of visitors, that I made my way to his door to say "welcome back". I greeted his parents and sat with them in the salon. Then the door opened and in walked Khader — very thin but now standing straight and at least a foot taller than me and yes he was different but not in the way I expected. There was a light in his eyes I hadn't seen before and a warmth in his attitude. I stood up to shake his hand and the next thing I knew my feet were inches off the floor and he was holding me in a bear hug. This was a new Khader, a Khader who knew Jesus's promise at first hand —

"I will never leave you nor forsake you".

Hebrews 13 verse 5.

On the night of his release the Captain had come to his cell and told him he was being taken to a prison in the desert. He picked up his Bible which had the wrapping paper from the piece of chocolate inside it and followed the Captain. When they got to the door the Captain told him to run, to go home to his family. Khader hadn't confessed because he hadn't done anything. He was released without being charged or tried or fined.

It was late at night, Khader did not know where he was. He had been blindfolded when they took him to prison. He was one hour and a half drive away from his home and there was no transportation. After knocking on several doors a family took him in, gave him a meal and let him stay on their couch until morning. Then they took him to the bus and gave him money for the fare home.

Khader was released on Monday evening and on the following Saturday, Bishara Awad from the Bible College and Solomon Douhne from Hope School, attended the monthly meeting of the Arab and Israeli believers and shared Khader's story of how the Lord had sent an angel to comfort Khader — an Israeli soldier. As they sat down, a young man stood up and simply said, "I was that soldier and I didn't know how the Lord used me". He later met Khader's parents and Khader's mother told me that the tears flowed freely at that meeting. As he was leaving, Khader's mother told the soldier — "Now I have three sons".

Although still not strong physically, Khader returned to his studies at the Bible College and completed his course. He now had a hunger in his heart to study Biblical subjects and obtain at least a BA so he could become a pastor and when an American lady offered to help pay his college fees he jumped at the chance and was accepted at the Evangelical Theological Seminary in Cairo. As he said farewell to his family he gave his mother the Bible she had sent him in prison and the wrapping paper from the piece of chocolate the soldier had given him and told her to guard his most treasured possessions until he returned.

He did return after gaining very high marks at the Seminary and he helped at the Bible College and in the Lutheran Church in Beit Jala until the Autumn of 1992.

It was a very special day when Khader took the Chapel at Hope School. His teachers were so proud of him and he preached a message the students will remember. His text was from Luke, Chapter 5 when Jesus preached from Simon's ship to the crowds on the shore and then told the disciple to launch out into the deep and when they did they caught a multitude of fish. Khader urged the students to follow Jesus, like the disciple, not to stand on the shore but to follow Him into the deep waters. He assured them that Jesus would never let them down — an assurance he could really testify to.

Is Khader still working on the West Bank? Not at the moment. Why? Well I guess the whole world has the saying, "In spring a young man's fancy lightly turns to thoughts of love".

Perhaps Khader's thoughts, one day in March 1992 when he was invited to a picnic at the Dead Sea might have "lightly turned to thoughts of love" but by the end of the day they definitely had. Thoughts that would culminate in a marriage ceremony held in Philadelphia, U.S.A. on 18 December 1992.

Who was it that captured Khader's thoughts on that Dead Sea picnic? She was a beautiful girl, as tall and slender as Khader himself, with a beautiful name, Grace. She was born in Jerusalem to Palestinian parents, the Rev. George and Frasina Kuttab. She was educated at the Friends School in Ramallah and then went with her family to live in the U.S.A. where she studied for a Nursing degree, specialising in Intensive Care patients. Once qualified she gave a few days a week to voluntary nursing in a clinic for those who needed medical help but couldn't afford it. How did she come to be at that picnic at the Dead Sea?

Her sister, who organised the picnic is Lydia Kuttab Brenneman, a Co-Director of Hope School at that time. But Grace wasn't paying her sister a social visit. She was in Jerusalem on a special mission. She had come with Operation Smile, a group of doctors and nurses from the U.S.A. organised by Jim and Linda Ryan, who gave their services and time free of charge to specifically perform cleft palette and hare lip operations on children whose parents could not normally afford to pay for the operation. They also operated on club feet. Operation Smile descended on the Augusta Victoria Hospital on the Mt. of Olives in March 1992 and Grace came to act as a nurse and translator. Operation Smile was a huge success and Grace, who already had a beautiful smile returned to the U.S.A. with not only a smile on her face but in her heart to prepare for her wedding with Khader.

They are both now living in Philadelphia and in September, 1993, Khader will continue his studies at the seminary in order to gain his M.A.

Yes, tears of sorrow and of joy are a common human experience and so is laughter. Not only I, but many of my English friends who have visited me, have been amazed at the capacity of the Palestinian people to laugh in the midst of suffering and loss of freedom. One comes away from a visit to their homes with the memory of smiling faces but they are a people who know the full meaning of Ecclesiastes 3 verse 4, for them there is —

> *"A time to weep and a time to laugh, a time to mourn and a time to dance."*

Chapter 13

The Ways Of The Lord Are Right

Hosea 14 verse 9

On Wednesday, 31st October, 1990 I received a Work Permit dated until 31st October 1991. I could stay in the Land one more year and I inwardly relaxed. No more trips to the various offices for at least eleven months and I could spend Christmas in Bethlehem. The visa and work permit situation was settled for a while.

Then on Monday 5th November I decided to call my oldest cousin Doris in Mansfield, England. She had been on my mind as I knew she was going through a difficult time nursing an aunt of ours. In the middle of the conversation I asked her if she would be going to spend Christmas with her sister, which she usually did. Doris then told me that Aunty Ivy was very, very frail and couldn't be left alone so she would not be able to leave her. Our Aunt was 78 years old at this time and Doris in her early seventies. Without thinking I said, "Would you like me to come and spend Christmas with you?" I could almost audibly hear her sigh of relief as she said, "Oh, that would be lovely". I finished the conversation by saying, "Well, I will have to see if I can get a re-entry visa, so that I don't lose my work permit and if I can, then I will come".

The next day Brice, the School Principal, had to go to the Military Governor's Office and so I asked him to enquire if I could get a re- entry visa without losing my work permit. He came back to say that I couldn't get a re-entry visa but that my Work Permit would remain valid and that on my return to the country I would be able to get a new visa. So my plans to celebrate Christmas in Bethlehem were put aside.

I caught the flight to London Heathrow on 19th December and finally arrived at the home of my cousin on 21st December. As I sipped my welcome cup of tea and looked at my aunt, so frail and unable to do anything for herself, I knew I was in the place the Lord wanted me to be and I was awed yet again of how God shows His love for us. To bring me all those miles to be with my cousin when she needed me. Her remarks on Christmas Day confirmed this. She was in the kitchen preparing the Christmas lunch and she looked at me and said, "If you hadn't come I would have been crying as I prepared the Christmas dinner and would have probably only made a sandwich anyway."

I returned to Bristol for a few days before my return flight booked for January 7th, to be confronted with television news bulletins announcing that Operation Desert Storm would be put into operation if Saddam Hussein did not comply with the U.N. deadline set for 15 January 1991. Friends kept telephoning to advise me not to return on the 7th but wait and see what happened. Within me I felt it was right to return but to reassure my friends, who filled our sitting room on the morning of 7th January, I called British Airways to confirm that the flight was on schedule and it was. Then I called the Foreign Office who assured me that as I had been living on the West Bank for eight years there was no reason why I shouldn't return. It was only tourists they were advising not to go. I hurriedly finished my packing and headed for Heathrow Airport.

As I checked in I began to realise that things weren't quite the same as usual. I was told that the flight would be delayed one hour and that we would put down at Athens in order to change crew so that they could fly directly back to London from Tel Aviv. That meant we would be 2 hours later landing so I telephoned friends and asked them to inform the School that I would be 2 hours late. I had arranged for my neighbour, Ibrahim Ghanem, to meet me in his taxi and I didn't want him to have to wait that long.

As we landed and stepped off the plane we were the only plane on the runway and as we came through the customs exit the airport was deserted, no taxis, no buses, only private individuals meeting their relatives from the plane. I looked around and there was no Ibrahim. This was most unusual as he could always be relied on to be punctual. The passengers quickly disappeared leaving me and one Arab lady alone in the deserted airport. I called the school and they assured me Ibrahim had been given the message. They told me to wait one hour and then call back if he still hadn't arrived. As I waited a few passengers came to check in on the return B.A. flight to London and I recognised another taxi driver from Beit Jala carrying suitcases for his passengers. I went up to him to ask if he would take me to Beit Jala and as soon as he saw me he said, "Ibrahim is being checked at the Gate, he told me to tell you to wait for him." So I sat down again. I had arrived at 7 a.m. and Ibrahim finally arrived at 10 a.m. He had his wife Suzanne and his boys Ishaac and Jabre with him. It was the first time they had been to the airport and were so excited that they were going to have a look around. They had arrived at the entrance at 6.30 a.m. and had been kept until 10 a.m. for security check and so after we had greeted each other Ibrahim said to them, "Quickly, get back into the taxi and let's go." They never did get to see the airport and we returned to Beit Jala without stopping. I was back but this time I realised things were far from normal.

The students at the School were still on Christmas vacation but we began to prepare for their return. As the deadline of 15 January drew nearer we were urged on radio and television to prepare a sealed room, with food and water available, in case war broke out. There was a frantic rush to buy mastik and sealing tape and the price of these items trebled.

On January 12th as I returned home from School, Suzanne from her apartment below mine, rang my doorbell and said Ibrahim had sent her to tell me that I was to move in with them and share their sealed room. It would have been impossible to seal my room in the Church and besides it would not have been good for me to stay alone. So I told her I would move in with them on Monday 14th January, the day before the deadline expired. Then I went with her to help get the room ready. We sealed the window tightly and criss crossed it with tape in case of bomb blast. I did half the window and

Ibrahim did the other half. Ishaac, his oldest son, watched us intently. I carefully put the tape making diamond shapes like a lattice window, Ibrahim was only concerned with protecting the glass and put his tape anyhow. Ishaac very seriously said, "Lynn's side is much nicer than yours Boppa". We laughed, how could you explain to a seven year old you weren't doing it to look nice but to protect from germ warfare and bomb blasts. We checked that we had all that was necessary in the room — glass bottles of water, food, first aid kit, bicarbonate of soda, a lamp, blankets, mattresses, radio, and rags to put over mouths if chemical gas came. I had an item which I knew should go in the room but was a little hesitant to suggest it. Being the holder of a British passport I had been issued with a gas mask, my Palestinian neighbours had not. They were eventually given them near the end of the war. I finally plucked up courage and told Ibrahim that I had it and suggested we hide it and one of us could use it if it became necessary. The kit also contained an injection to be used if a certain kind of gas was dropped.

I moved in with the Ghanem family on 14th January.

The 15th came and went, the 16th likewise and the 17th was a normal day and we occupied ourselves as usual. At about 2 a.m. in the morning I was woken by heavy knocking on the door and a voice shouting that missiles had hit Tel Aviv. We turned on the radio and were told to enter the sealed room. We carried the sleeping boys into the room and the five of us remained there the rest of the night listening to the radio. As daylight broke we were told it was safe to come out of the room but for occupants of the West Bank it was not safe to come out of their houses because a 24 hour curfew had been imposed.

We spent the next night of 18th January again in the sealed room and Tel Aviv was once more hit by missiles and again on the 19th January.

During the day time I helped to keep Ishaac and Jabre occupied, making craft things and playing games. There was no television programmes for the first two days, only news bulletins. On the morning of the 19th we heard a knock at the door and looking out of the window saw Suzanne's aunt who had crept through the olive groves to check if we were alright. She had brought us some cakes she had made. We unsealed the door and let her in.

After checking there were no soldiers around I took the opportunity of the open door to take the two boys up to my apartment for a break. We made some cakes and play-dough and had a game of table tennis before returning to their apartment. The boys insisted on taking the play- dough with them and when Ibrahim's eyes fell on it he pounced, "That's perfect for sealing doors," he said. So I had to make another batch.

In the afternoon I was in the kitchen and Suzanne switched on the television in the sitting room. She let out a shout of excitement and thinking the war was over, I rushed in to see. I couldn't believe my eyes, her excitement was caused because the TV was showing cartoons. She was so happy that there was something for the children to watch. We had only two boisterous boys to keep occupied in the confines of the house, it must have been a real headache for those with lots of children.

Sunday morning, 20th January dawned and I walked into the kitchen to see Ibrahim gazing out of the window. "What are you looking at?" I asked him. "The birds", he replied. "Oh are there some special ones", I asked. "I'm checking to see if they are alive, that way we will know if any gas has been dropped!"

Suzanne and I decided to bake some bread and then again we heard a knock at the door and it was Imm Basem, our landlady and neighbour come through the olive groves to see if we were alright. She spotted the play-dough and begged for some, so I gave her the recipe as well. It was much cheaper than tape and mastik. I should have thought of it before the curfew was imposed! I again took advantage of the open door to take the boys upstairs to my apartment for a change.

On Sunday afternoon we heard on the radio that the people of Bethlehem were to be allowed out for two hours to buy food. So being the next town everyone assumed the people of Beit jala would be the next allowed out. On the stroke of 2 p.m. everyone streamed out of their houses, shouting and greeting one another. Cars sped past to be the first to get to the market. As we climbed into Ibrahim's taxi the cars began to return and shouted to us to get back into the house. We were not being allowed out to buy food as the soldiers were shooting tear gas. So we walked back down the stairs into the house once more.

When I was in England, on the 1st January 1991, I decided that I would read through the Bible in a year and naturally began in Genesis. By January 18th I had reached Genesis Chapter 31. In spite of the curfew and war we were trying to continue life as normal so I opened my Bible that morning to read that Chapter. I stopped when I reached verse 3 —

> *"And the Lord said to Jacob, Return unto the land of thy fathers and to thy kindred and I will be with thee."*

My mind briefly re-acted with "Lord are these words for me today?" then I dismissed the thought, the words were for Jacob not me and I continued reading until I reached verse 13 and stopped again...

> *"now arise get thee out from this land and return to the land of thy kindred."*

I pondered on these words all day.

On Saturday morning, January 19th, I looked at the verse on my calendar, it said,

> *"Whatever He says to you, do it." John 2 v 5.*

Then I picked up my Bible to continue reading in Genesis, Chapter 32 and stopped at verse 9. There again were the instructions,

> *"Return to thy country, and to thy kindred and I will deal well with thee."*

This time I did more than think and ponder, I prayed. "Lord if this is from You, You will have to send someone to help me. You know I cannot leave the house because of the curfew and we have no telephone!"

The next day was Sunday and just as I entered the house after our attempt to go out to buy food, there was a knock on the door. It was Bishara Awad from the Bible College, come to see if I was alright. I told him I thought the Lord was telling me to go home and he responded, "You can't, there aren't any planes." "That is it then", I said, "But please check." He said he would and left. The whole visit was less than 5 minutes.

On Monday, 21st January at 12 noon, they announced on the radio that the people of Beit Jala could leave their homes for 2 hours to buy food. First I went with Ibrahim, Suzanne and the boys to the market and the whole of the village was there. I went to the Pharmacy, a tiny little shop, and it was packed to the doors. People were frantic to buy baby food, milk powder and medicines, not knowing when they would again be let out of their houses. Suzanne managed to buy some vegetables and some meat, though they were not very fresh. We had left bread to rise in the house. Then we headed for Hope School so I could telephone my family to let them know I was alright. I never arrived there for on the way up the hill I met Attallah Esawi, Pastor of the Church of God in Beit Jala. He stopped his van and walked over to our car and said, "Go home, quickly. Paul, from the Mt. of Olives Church is on his way to take you to the airport." I returned to my apartment and gathered my personal papers, passport etc. The neighbours had heard I was leaving and came into the apartment. Some of them in tears as they didn't want me to leave. They were urging me to pack a suitcase but I said, "No, I have clothes in England". One asked if she could borrow my electric fire to keep the baby warm as they had little kerosene, another asked for my radio and then there was Paul at the door. "Where are you taking her", they all cried. He laughed and said, "To England."

Then we were on our way to Jerusalem. Paul stopped at the road block to ask the soldiers if he could bring in food when the curfew was lifted next and they told him he could.

I turned to him and again asked him where he was taking me. "To Jerusalem", he said, "You will probably have to wait 3 or 4 days before you can leave, there is a waiting list for flights." Now I wished I had packed at least one change of clothing and my toothbrush!

However within ten minutes of arriving at the Church of God on the Mt. of Olives, the telephone rang. It was the Travel Agency to say there was a seat on the 5.15 p.m. flight the next day. Would I collect and pay for my ticket in the morning. Turning to Paul, I asked him how I could get the cash to pay. The ticket was £264 and I had a little over £300 in my bank account, but would have to cash a cheque. Paul responded by telling me he would take me to the money changer's home first thing in the morning but he wasn't sure what the rate of exchange would be, so I decided to write a cheque for £300 to be sure.

As we pulled up outside the money changer's house the next morning, Paul told me to stay in the van and he would take the cheque in as the money changer knew him. He was gone quite a while and as he climbed into the van he handed me a wad of shekels. "I don't know how much there is", he said, "I had a hard time to get him to change the cheque and he said, "Doesn't the lady know there is a war on?" As we stopped at the Travel Agency Paul said, "If you don't have enough money, I have 100 shekels on me." The lady in the Travel Agency gave me my ticket, impressed upon me I must stay by the telephone as the flight arrangements could be changed. I handed her the wad of money and held my breath. She counted it and handed me back 3 shekels in change. There was just enough.

We returned to the Mt. of Olives to await the time of my departure for the airport. Things were going well but there was still a little niggle in my mind. "Would I have enough sterling to buy a bus ticket from London Heathrow to Bristol?" I knew by the time I arrived at Heathrow it would be late at night and the ticket agency and money exchanges would be closed which meant I would have to pay the bus driver direct because he wouldn't take a cheque. I needn't have worried.

I telephoned Hope School. Brice and Lydia, who had permission to come to Jerusalem to buy chicken food for the Hope School hens, said they would call in to see me and bring in the School mail for me to take to England and deal with there. Amongst the mail were some personal envelopes for me. Christmas cards from people who hadn't known I had decided to spend Christmas in England. As I had time to kill before going to the airport I decided I would open the mail. In three of my personal envelopes I found a £5 note — £15 altogether and enough to buy my ticket from Heathrow to Bristol.

I arrived at Ben Gurion Airport at 3.30 p.m. and checked in. Then waited and waited. The time for the scheduled departure 5.15 p.m. had come and gone. The runway was completely deserted, not a truck or plane in sight and it was raining heavily. Inside the terminal there were just the people on my flight and a few early arrivals for the only other flight out, the 8 p.m. flight to Toronto. As we waited speculation was going on as to where our plane was. Finally just after 6 o'clock we were told we could board but there was still no plane on the runway. Still we gathered up our bags, walked down the stairs to the edge of the runway to find one airport bus waiting to take us to the plane. By the time it was my turn to board the bus it was full and I was left waiting on the edge of the runway thinking that the next bus would follow on behind normally. It didn't, they were only using one bus. So I stood there waiting. It was dark, foggy and raining hard and I felt desolate, wondering if I had done the right thing. My tears were mixed with the raindrops. Through the rain I saw the glow of headlights. Thinking it was the airport bus returning I looked up to see a truck (that had obviously guided the plane in) driving past. As I watched it my eyes focused on the big bold letter on top of the truck — FOLLOW ME — and following behind was the airport bus.

I got on with my fellow passengers and drove out to the plane which had been carefully hidden. As I climbed the steps into the plane my heart was sad but I knew I was in the Lord's will and that was all that mattered. Finally the plane took off somewhere around 6.30 p.m. and I settled into my seat.

After supper had been served I saw a smartly dressed man coming down the aisle giving out papers. I thought he was a steward giving out immigration forms. He wasn't. He gave the paper to the gentleman sitting next to me in the aisle seat who read it then smilingly turned and gave it to me. I couldn't believe my eyes, it was the man's testimony of how the Lord Jesus had healed him of alcohol problems, physical problems and a death wish. It ended with the words, "Why not make your eternal decision now" and a prayer of commitment. As I looked at my fellow passengers, most of them Jewish and fleeing to the safety of relatives in England, I saw smiles on their faces. No one tried to stop the man or remonstrated with him as he gave out the leaflets.

On arrival at Heathrow I made my way to a cold deserted bus station. It was approx. 10 p.m. and I knew there was a bus due for Bristol at 10.40 p.m. No one else was waiting for a bus to go anywhere, I was the only passenger and I was tired and weary and shivering in the cold January night. As I waited a bus arrived bound for Cardiff and pulled in. The driver assured me the Bristol bus was on its way. As I was talking to the bus driver, a young mother, with her two children and a trolley full of luggage came towards the bus. I recognised her from the departure lounge at Tel Aviv. She asked the bus driver, "Is this bus going to Cardiff?" "It is", he replied and the relief on her face spoke volumes.

As the driver was putting her luggage into the bus my Bristol bus arrived. I boarded and told the driver I didn't have a ticket. "Neither do I" was his response, "You had better go and ask the Cardiff driver if he has any". He had and as I turned to get off his bus I looked at the young Jewish mother and her children and said "Shalom". She looked at me startled and I quickly re-assured her by saying, "You were on the same plane as me from Tel Aviv". Her response was not only for herself but for all those I had left behind, my Palestinian friends and neighbours and the Israelis, all locked in their sealed rooms waiting for scud attacks and chemical warfare. The mother said, "I didn't see anyone on the plane, I am so afraid". A fear that was justified as I stepped off the bus in Bristol. My nephew, Dave, who had come to meet me said "Have you heard the news? The scuds again hit Tel Aviv at 7 p.m. this time killing 3 people, injuring many and making many homeless. We had missed the attack by a matter of 30 minutes.

It wasn't long before I knew why the Lord had told me to return unto the land of my fathers and my kindred. I called my cousin Doris to ask how she and my aunt were. I was told that my aunt was in a nursing home and that Doris had been given a small flat in a warden controlled complex for the elderly. She had one month to pack up her belongings and furniture from the rented house which had been the home of our Grandparents. The home I had been taken to from the hospital immediately after my mother's death, at the age of two weeks. Could I go and help her?

Once again the Lord had brought me back to help my cousin when she needed me the most. The lot fell to me to put into packing cases the things Doris wanted to take to her new home and sort out the things to be given to charity. She needed help to choose the pieces of furniture she wanted to take and find homes for the furniture there wasn't room for in her new small flat.

Removal day came and with the help of other family members, the last of the furniture and boxes were loaded onto the van and I was left with another cousin to take up the carpets to be collected by someone else. I returned with a family friend, two days later to sweep and wash the floors and for the last time turn the key in the door of the house that had been my family's home for at least 60 years. A family that had loved and cared for me "From my mother's arms".

I helped Doris settle into her new home, which was located only ten minutes walking distance from the nursing home where our aunt was now being looked after. The I returned to Bristol to spend Easter with my family. My sister Mary and her husband Mike had come from Canada to visit us.

Operation Desert Storm was over. Hope School had re-opened but it was not quite time for me to return. Physically and emotionally I was tired and Hope School had a temporary secretary in my place. Mirth Brenneman (the Principal's mother) with her husband John had very courageously volunteered to go to the School to support Brice and Lydia in that difficult period, so I decided to remain in England a little longer.

Not only in England, for on 10 April 1991 I left with Janet Angle representing Friends of Hope School, to spend a lovely week in Iceland. We met Hope School sponsors in Rekjavik and the Westmann Islands and spoke in the Betel Church on Westmann and the Filadelfia Church in Rekjavik. On my last day in Rekjavik, Olafur Johannsson who had invited me to make the visit and who organised the Friends of Hope School in Iceland, presented me with a cheque for $1,000 for the school. Besides the cheque my luggage held two other items presented to me during the visit. One given to me by Bev and Einar Gislason, was a wooden plaque showing Jesus, the Good Shepherd, surrounded by a flock of sheep and holding a lamb in His arms. Bev and Einar had the plaque hanging on the wall of their apartment and one evening as we had supper with them, they asked me how I had gone to work at Hope School. I pointed to the plaque and said, "That is my testimony — Feed My lambs". On my last evening in Rekjavik, Olafur called to collect us to go to supper with all the sponsors and he gave me a package from Bev and Einar. Imagine my surprise on unwrapping the package that they had given me, to find the wooden plaque with their love.

The other gift in my suitcase was given to me by another sponsor, Gudbjartur Thorleifsson. He had called to ask if I would collect a gift for the student he sponsored and said he had left it at the Church bookstore. The girl in the store handed me the package from Gudbjartur who is a jeweller and then gave me two neatly wrapped boxes, one for me and one for Janet. On opening them we found necklaces made of pieces of volcanic lava covered in 22 carat gold.

Hope School and Bethlehem seemed a long way off but now I was refreshed in body and spirit and it was time to return. Once more I boarded the British Airways flight bound for Ben Gurion Airport, Tel Aviv. It was Saturday, May 4th. Looking back over the first four months of 1991 I knew that although there were many things I didn't understand, without a doubt "The ways of the Lord were right..."

Chapter 14
Christmas in Bethlehem

Laila Tal Milad Yomma hal bogdou
In the evening of Christmas is gone the hatred
Laila Tal Milad tuzzhiro-l-ardo
In the evening of Christmas is blossoming the earth
laila Tal Milad tud fano-l-harbo
In the evening of Christmas is obliterated the war
Laila Tal Milad yan bothol - hobbo
In the evening of Christmas is flowing the love.

My favourite Arabic Christmas song sums up what we all feel Christmas is about. Brotherly love, goodwill towards men, peace on earth.

Before I lived in Bethlehem, Christmas Eve in the Church of England was special. I thought of Mary and Joseph, the donkey, the inn and the birth of baby Jesus. I didn't dwell on the long journey Mary and Joseph had been forced to make for the Census being taken, the fact that they had to beg for accommodation, that the town would be filled with soldiers nor even the fact that Herod, soon after Jesus's birth, would order the killing of all little boys aged from birth to 2 years, in the area. My Western mind dwelt on the "nice" things that happened that first Christmas. The reality of it all didn't sink in, although I always had a sense of wonder and awe as I read and listened to the Christmas story.

Yes there was reality in Bethlehem 2,000 years ago, but there was also wonder, awe, worship and the adoration of the shepherds and Wise men. At Christmastime in Bethlehem today there is still reality, wonder, awe, worship and adoration.

Let me share some extracts from Christmas newsletters I wrote:

1982

We had the first heavy rain of the winter a few weeks ago, it lasted four days and was very cold, so it gave me a foretaste of things to come. The houses here are not geared for winter. With only calor gas, paraffin heaters and wood burning stoves, heating is not good. One thing the cold weather has made me realise is that the carol *"In the bleak mid winter, frosty wind made moan"*, is not out of keeping because Bethlehem in December can be bleak, especially when the cold east wind blows.

I experienced my first fall of snow in Bethlehem on New Year's day and sharing about that was my answer to friends who wrote in their Christmas cards that first year — "Aren't you lucky to be spending Christmas in Bethlehem in the sunshine!"

1983 and 1985

I will be in Bethlehem on Christmas Eve to celebrate at the Programme of Christmas Lights at Bethlehem Bible College which is situated halfway between Manger Square and the Shepherds Fields. Christians, Pilgrims and Tourists to Bethlehem from all over the world will gather at the Bible College to worship and praise the living God.

It will be a little different in Manger Square with soldiers, check points and tickets only, to get into the Church of the Nativity. However, there will be choirs from all around the world singing Christmas songs in the square and this year (1985) one special choir will be taking part, the Bethlehem Bible College Choir.

Down the hill though, in the Shepherds Fields the atmosphere will be the same as it was that wonderful night when Jesus was born. It will be quiet and calm with the stars shining brightly and a nip in the air and something special about the place that words cannot describe.

The Christmas of 1985 I had my friend Pauline Illsley staying with me and that Christmas Eve we walked to the Shepherds Fields, spent a time of quietness in the Cave and Chapel of the Franciscans and then in the fading light climbed the hill back to the Bible College. Inside the building the lights were blazing and people filled each room. As we entered we were given a Programme which said:

WELCOME TO THE CHRISTMAS CELEBRATION

PLACE:	*Bethlehem Bible College* *Shepherds Field Road* *Bethlehem*
TIME:	*Tuesday, December 24, 1985* *5.30p.m. until 12.00a.m. midnight*
PROGRAMME	
5.30 - 6.00	*Refreshments – Welcome– Christmas Songs*
6.00 – 6.30	*Bible Readings – The Christmas Story in different languages.*
6.30 – 7.00	*Bethlehem Bible College Choir*
7.00 – 7.30	*Testimonies by the Community*
7.30 – 7.40	*Prayer and Praise*
7.40 – 8.00	*Sisters of Mary – Special Presentation*
8.00 – 8.30	*Refreshments – Intermission*
8.30 – 9.15	*Puppet Christmas Story with Jerry and Mary Rausin* *"Mary had a little lamb"*
9.15 – 9.25	*Group Singing*
9.25 – 10.00	*Christmas Message – Rev. Michael Peters*
10.00 – 10.20	*Christmas Drama*
10.20 – 10.40	*Group Presentations*
10.40 – 11.00	*Refreshments – Intermission*
11.00 – 11.20	*Christmas Message – Rev. Martin Kielwein*
11.20 –11.35	*Special Programme*
11.35 – 12.00	*Worship in Song – Candle Light Choir*
Please Note:	*1 Counselling, prayer and helps room will be open all evening* *2 Video room will be open all evening*

This is the perfect night to repent and follow Jesus:
HE CAME FOR YOU

These celebrations had begun in 1983 through the initiative of the Sisters of Mary. All denominations took part including Messianic Believers. the aim was to provide a place of welcome, warmth and worship in Bethlehem on Christmas Eve but most of all to fulfil the words printed on the bottom of the Programme:

"This is the perfect night to repent and follow Jesus:
HE CAME FOR YOU..."

At the end of the first Christmas Eve Celebrations in 1983, Alex Awad and I were the last people in the building and we were just about to lock the door and return to Alex and Brenda's home in Beit Sahour (where I was spending Christmas) when a group of young men and women returned. They told us there was no transport back to Jerusalem and could they stay the night at the college. They promised to leave the next morning. So Alex organised mattresses for the floors of two classrooms and looking at me said: "We can hardly say 'No' on Christmas Eve in Bethlehem!"

Sadly the Celebrations could no longer be held after the Intefada started in December 1987.

1986

Ring out those bells tonight
Bethlehem, Bethlehem,
Follow that star tonight
Bethlehem, Bethlehem.

After four years I still get a thrill when I hear the bells of Bethlehem ringing. The bells of the Church of Nativity are the joyous ones that thrill my heart the most as they ring out the good news that Jesus Christ is born.

Christmas celebrations seem to be the same the world over, I was involved in two Church programmes and was a spectator at the School concert. We had our usual Christmas play for parents at the Beit Jala Church. My class acted the Christmas story and the younger children sang songs and shared Christmas verses. There were over 130 children plus parents, so it was a tight squeeze and absolute chaos reigned for half an hour whilst the Christmas gifts were distributed, but the happy smiles made it all worth it. The little girls who received the dolls sent out by my friends from Trinity Tabernacle Bristol, were so happy.

The programme at the Church of God on the Mt. of Olives was much quieter and somehow very special this year. We did the Christmas story in mime then sang a medley of Christmas songs and ended by lighting a candle on a birthday cake for Jesus, made in Bethlehem.

The School concert was very well done and it was held in the village hall so more people could attend. The School Choir sang Christmas songs, there were Bible readings and a Christmas play. I was proud of myself for recognising it as a modern version of "A Christmas Carol". I hadn't been in on the rehearsals so didn't know what they were doing. The programme ended with a performance by the Beit Jala Scouts Pipe and Drum Band, many of whom were our students — a stirring end indeed!

1988

O little town of Bethlehem
How still we see thee lie...

The streets of Bethlehem are still and silent today, a forced silence of strikes and curfews on this first anniversary of the Intefada. The town is busy from 9a.m. to noon when people go about their business and housewives hurriedly buy food for their families. Then the streets become deserted. The same situation applies in Beit Jala. High above Bethlehem and Beit Jala is Hope School. Normally a place of busy activity but for the past 5 months also a place of silence, due to closure by the army. Not only are the streets silent, but many homes are silent too, missing the voice of a loved one.

Sharif our 12 year old student misses the voice of his father, killed by a bullet in March; Imm Jeries, our cook, her daughter-in-law and grandchildren miss the voice of their beloved son, husband and father — also shot dead...

There will be no Christmas celebrations this year for the people of Bethlehem and Beit Jala. No celebration in Bethlehem Bible College on Christmas Eve when Arab and Jewish believers usually meet together to worship Jesus.

There are a few hopeful signs — the School may open on 11th December; my work permit application is being considered and so it would seem that for the time being my star is still shining over Bethlehem. Please remember us all in Bethlehem this Christmas Eve and please pray for us...

The School did in fact re-open on 11 December and the week before Christmas I went with Laren Lyebarger, our American volunteer, to take some of the boys to their homes for the holidays. It was a hazardous journey and I think we were both very relieved to get back safely to the School. It was also a worthwhile journey. We visited the home of Sharif, the boy whose father was killed. A very poor home with no furnishings and the mother, looking no more than a child herself was now a widow with nine children to care for. Three of her sons are at Hope School and as we were leaving she held me tightly and said "Please take care of my boys". I left in tears and although I said, "Of course we would take care for her boys", it is not easy to keep a promise like that in our situation and so I would like to ask you to join me in taking care of them by praying for their protection, daily.

1989

Once again we find our way to Bethlehem and listen for the angel's song, *"Glory to God in the highest"*...

Sadly I haven't found my way to Bethlehem too many times this year, because of the continuing situation.

"Though we are pressed on every side by troubles, we are not crushed or broken. We are perplexed because we don't know why things happen as they do, but we don't give up. We are hunted down, but God never abandons us. We get knocked down, but we get up again and keep going. Though our bodies are dying, our inner strength in the Lord is growing every day. These troubles and sufferings of ours are, after all, quite small and won't last very long. Yet this short time of distress will result in God's richest blessing upon us for ever and ever. So we do not look at what we can see at this moment with troubles all around us, but we look forward to the joys of heaven which we have not yet seen. The troubles will soon be over but the joys to come will last forever..."

2 Corinthians

The saying, "No news is good news" is often true but I am sorry to say it is not so of the situation here. Many of you write that you are not getting reports and so feel things are better. They are not and I would like to ask you to continue praying for us. Your prayers are needed more than ever, for the students and staff of Hope School, the Bethlehem Bible College and for me personally. So please put us high on your 1990 prayer list.

1991

This was a personal Christmas for me with celebrations at the School, a Christmas play and gifts for the students, Sunday School celebrations in Beit Jala and a supper with the teen-agers. I attended the House of Hope for the Blind and Handi-capped Christmas programme with Aunty May Ladah and the children presented the Christmas story. That was a special occasion. Also a Christmas Lunch at the Church of God on the Mt. of Olives.

But no visit to Bethlehem for me or my Palestinian Christian friends and neighbours in Beit Jala who stayed in the security of their homes to celebrate the birth of our Lord Jesus Christ.

We all longed for the words of the Arabic Carol to become reality:

Laila tal Milad yomma hal bogdou
In the evening of Christmas is gone the hatred
Laila Tal Milad tuzzhiro - l-ardo
In the evening of Christmas is blossoming the earth
Laila Tal milad tud fano-l-harbo
In the evening of Christmas is obliterated the war
Laila tal milad yan botho l-hobbo
In the evening of Christmas is flowing the love.
Aindama nasqui aatchana kassa ma nakuunu filmilad
When we give the thirsty one a glass (of water) we have Christmas
Aindama naksi aoriana thoubahobb na kuunu filmilad
When we put on the naked a robe of love we'll have Christmas

Aindama nokafkif oddomog fil auyuun nakuunu filmilad
When we wipe out the tears in the eyes (of the sad) we'll have Christmas
Ainda ma nafro shul qulubabirra ja nakuunu filmilad
When we fill in the hearts hope we'll have Christmas

Aindama o Qabbilu ra fiqi dona aich akuunu filmilad
When we kiss our friend without grudge it will be Christmas
Ainama famuulu fi a ruhu lintiqam a kuuna filmilad
When dies the spirit of revenge it will be Christmas
Ainda ma yoromado biqalbi aljafa a kuunu filmilad
When extracted from my heart the enmity it will be Christmas
Ainda ma ta dhobonafsi fi kiyanilla a kuuna filmilad
When melts my soul in the person of God it will be Christmas.

Chapter 15
The Lord is MY Shepherd

I shall not want. He maketh me to lie down in green pastures. He leadeth me beside the still waters. He restoreth my soul...
Psalm 23

My favourite tune for the 23rd Psalm is the Brother James Air. It repeats the stanza — He leadeth me, He leadeth me...

Yes I returned to Hope School on 4 May 1991 after the Gulf War, refreshed physically but still in need of a longer period of rest for my mind and spirit. For ten years I had been feeding His lambs and had reached the point when I needed feeding myself. Not only is the Lord Jesus Christ my shepherd, He is the Good Shepherd and knows His sheep by name and knows their every need. He knew I was in need of rest, refreshment and spiritual food and so He began to slowly lead me to the point when I knew it was His will for me to leave Hope School and my Palestinian friends and neighbours. Slowly... Leading... He is the Good Shepherd, He doesn't rush or push His sheep, He slowly leads them to fresh pastures.

Since June 1990 I had been very much concerned about the Girl's meeting at the Church of God. Claude Abu Dayyeh who had been my translator and helper for several years left on 7th June 1990, to take up a scholarship at Messiah College in Pennsylvania, U.S.A. It had been my desire that Claude would eventually take over the Girl's work, but the Lord had other plans for her. I still felt it would be better for a local believer to run the work and began to pray about this. Then on June 23rd 1991 I went to the Church of God workers retreat at Betel Barraka near Hebron. At the retreat was Anna Yerimien from Bethlehem who had just returned from the Church of God Bible College in North Carolina, U.S.A.

Anna had been involved in the Youth Work at the Beit Jala Church of God before going to Bible College and she had also completed a two year course at the Church of God European Bible Seminary. As I passed Anna on the stairs I knew I had to ask her to take over my girls, so I stopped and told her that I would like to speak to her when she had some free time. We eventually got together two days later and when I asked her if she would be willing to take over the girl's ministry, the look on her face spoke volumes. She told me that back in the U.S.A. she had started to pray about her return and as to what she should do. She had a strong desire to work with the teenage girls but kept thinking "I can't do that, that is Sister Lynn's class". We both laughed, me with relief and Anna with joy at being given her heart's desire. I continued taking the meetings until August 1991 and the last meeting was special. Each girl had memorised the Lord's prayer and it was a precious moment as we prayed it together in Arabic and English.

The ladies meetings had become less frequent as it was difficult to arrange a suitable time to get together with strikes, curfews, road closures etc., though we did meet individually in each other's homes. It seemed the time had come to assess the meetings and it was decided to await the return of Pastor Attallah Esawi and his wife Hilda from the U.S.A. and to begin again through the Church. I was very moved when Imm Basem, who had attended the meetings, came to visit me when she heard the news that I was to leave. She looked at me and said, "I am going to tell you something now that I haven't told you before. You don't know it but you taught me to trust the Lord."

The thought of leaving Hope School and especially the students was the hardest thing I had to face and come to terms with. Changes had taken place during 1991. Bishara Awad had relinquished the Chairmanship of the School Board and a new committee had been elected and there were changes that I didn't find easy to come to terms with. As I had always said that it was the Lord that had brought me to Hope School and that I couldn't leave until He showed me it was time to leave, I knew I had to seek His will in this. In my quiet time on 15th October 1991, I asked Him specifically to make it clear if He wanted me to continue at Hope School. Again, slowly but surely, He showed me through Scripture and circumstances, that it was indeed time for me to leave.

From November 1991 to May 1992 the Scriptures came:

> *"Have I not commanded you. Be strong and of good courage, do not be frightened, neither be dismayed. The Lord your God is with you wherever you go."*
>
> *Joshua 1 v 9*

> *For I know the plans I have for you. Plans to give you a hope and a future.*
>
> *Jeremiah 29 v 11*

> *"Up, begone, this is no more your land and home. Your king will go before you. The Lord leads on."*
>
> *Micah 2 v 10*

> *"He determined the times set before them and the exact places where they should live."*
>
> *Acts 17 verses 25 & 26*

> *"Here we have no continuing city but we seek one to come."*
>
> *Hebrews 13 v 14*

> *"Behold I will do a new thing, now it shall spring forth, shall ye not know it? I will even make a way in the wilderness and rivers in the desert."*
>
> *Isaiah 43 v 19*

> *"And the Lord said... Return unto the land of thy fathers and to thy kindred and I will be with thee."*
>
> *Genesis 31 v 3*

> *"My presence shall go with thee and I will give thee rest."*
>
> *Exodus 33 v 14*

These verses and many more until finally on Friday the 1st of May 1992, I wrote my resignation and gave it to Brice Brenneman, the Principal.

Tuesday 2nd June was scheduled as the last day of the 1991/92 School year and I booked my ticket to return to England on Tuesday the 23rd June.

With the sadness of farewells my remaining time in the land was difficult. It was made easier by lots of visitors from England and by preparation for the celebrations of Hope School's 30th Anniversary and Graduation ceremony, plus the Graduation Ceremony at Bethlehem Bible College. However June 23rd arrived far too soon and once more I found myself in the early hours of the morning at Ben Gurion airport awaiting the flight to London, not knowing if or when I would be returning. My loved ones in Beit Jala and Bethlehem I knew were clinging to one of the verses I had been given...

> *"I am with you and will watch over you wherever you go and I will bring you back to this land."*
>
> *Genesis 28 v 15*

As I had begun to seek the Lord about my future I kept getting the word Sabbatical so I decided to look it up in the dictionary and read -

Sabbatical — *a period of leave granted at intervals to university professors, missionaries etc. for study and travel.*

The more I thought about it the more it seemed right for me to take a Sabbatical rest. I wasn't so sure if it was to study, but to travel and visit with family and friends seemed good. There was another thought drifting in and out of my head, put there by the Lord of that I was sure. I didn't really know how to come to grips with it so I kept putting it on one side. It was to write a book.

Whilst I was home in England in June 1990 I visited with Malcolm and Chris Neale and spoke at the Church they Pastor in Buttershaw, Bradford. Before the morning service I shared a prayer with some of the congregation and one of the members Nellie Summerscales, prayed for me personally. A prayer that moved me very much. After the service I thanked Nellie for her prayer and she told me she wanted so much to come and hear me speak again at the evening service but as she lived away from the Church it was difficult. The Church Secretary, Hilda Whitehead heard Nellie and suggested she spend the day with her and she would then bring Nellie to the evening service and take her home. Nellie was so pleased. After the evening service, when most people had gone home, Nellie walked towards me from the back of the room and as she reached me she said, "Lynn, you have to write a book and you have to call it HOPE." I laughed and said, "If I ever do Nellie it will be dedicated to You."

The seed was sown.

The Lord began to water it:

> *"Go now, write it on a tablet for them, note it in a book that for days to come it may be an everlasting witness."* *Isaiah 30 v 8*
>
> *"Write on a scroll what you see and send it to the... Churches."*
>
> *Rev. 1 v 10*

I prayed, "Father, if You want me to write a book, I ask you for help as I don't even know where to begin."

Back in England in August 1992 and lying sleepless on my bed in the early hours of the morning, came the song from Sound of Music — "Lets begin at the very beginning, that's a very good place to start."

The beginning for me was when I lay as a helpless babe in an incubator, denied the bonding so much talked about these days as necessary from the moment of birth, because my mother lay sick unto death in her bed beside me. All that was soon to be changed when the Lord placed me in the arms of a "new" mother who would bestow upon me the love I had been denied for a short while. As these thoughts drifted through my mind in those early morning hours, the seed took root and I knew I had to get on with the task and write the book but with a more meaningful title. It came from the words of the hymn — Now thank we all our God -"Who from our mother's arms". Nellie's title of Hope was to be the sub-title, which is also the Hope School verse —

> *"For Thou O Lord art my Hope, my trust O Lord from my youth."*
>
> *Psalm 71 v 5*

There were two commitments to be completed before I could begin the work. The first was to act as hostess, together with Colin Piper and Chris Curtis from the George Muller Foundation to five Hope School students — Na'eela Sarras, Abir Sarras, Sana Sa-idy, Abbas Othman and Nabil Rabaya and their teacher, George Abu Dayeh, who had been invited to spend three weeks in England as guests of Bristol School Christian Unions under the auspices of the Foundation.

The Group arrived on 20th August, 1992 and stayed until 12th September. Three very hectic, fun packed and moving weeks. For me it was awesome as well. I never in my wildest dreams thought I would have Hope School students sleeping, eating and fellowshipping together in my family home in Bristol. Nor taking part in the morning service at my home church of St. Matthews, Cotham. It was a privilege and a blessing. The students had been chosen because of their academic achievements. They had gained the highest marks in the final school examinations. Na-eela Sarras had gained the highest marks in the Commercial School Section in the whole West Bank. They were a credit to Hope School and wonderful ambassadors for the Palestinian people. I was so proud of them and thanked God for letting me have this time with them in my land.

All good things come to an end however and it was a bleak moment for us all as we said "Good bye" at Gatwick airport. As I waved my farewell I committed each one of them into God's keeping.

Whilst the group was in Bristol I took Abir Sarras to have afternoon tea with Nina Cox, her sponsor in Bristol. Nina had visited us at Hope School and had a real concern for Abir and the students at the School. During our conversation, Nina asked me what my plans were for the future and I shared about writing a book. On my return home and later that evening, the telephone rang and it was Nina. She told me she had a friend who was a publisher and if I would like to telephone her we could arrange a meeting.

The publisher was Anne Hodkinson from The Friendly Press. She and her husband Brian were wardens of the Religious Society of Friends (Quaker) Meeting House, which was just a few streets away from my home in Bristol. I literally could walk there in a few minutes. I telephoned Anne and arranged to meet with her in October after my return from a visit to my sister in Canada. This was the second commitment I had before I could get down to writing.

My sister Chris and I flew out to Toronto on Wednesday, 16th September to spend two weeks with our sister Mary and her husband Mike at their cottage home on the Trent River at Hastings, Ontario.

The beauty of our surroundings, the river, the trees beginning to be tinted with autumn colours, the wild flowers, the blue herons, blue jays, humming birds and chipmunks, the sunshine, wind and rain, all had a calming effect upon me.

I was able to rest and relax and at last begin to unwind and in the quietness and peace pour out my heart to the Lord.

A few days before our return to England the Lord showed me my next two steps. I was to have a Season of Rest and very clearly I was to get on with the book.

> *"And the Lord said (unto Moses) write this for a memorial in a book and rehearse it in the ears of (Joshua)."*
>
> *Exodus 17 v 14*

So I put together my thoughts concerning the book on paper. I put my Photograph albums of Hope School,Bethlehem Bible College and Church of God into a bag, together with a cassette of my testimony and I headed around the corner to the Friendly Press office and Anne Hodkinson. She sounded interested, told me to go away and write a few chapters and let her have them — then we would see.

On a day in mid January 1993 I duly deposited the first five chapters of the manuscript on her desk and went back home to await her verdict. The telephone rang at 8 p.m. and I heard the words "I like it, give me more".

A new era was opening up for me. I was on my way to becoming an authoress. I couldn't really take it in.

One suggestion Anne made was, that it would help if I knew of someone who could write a foreword for me. Immediately and without a thought I said, "Brother Andrew from Open Doors." I had met Brother Andrew when he visited Bishara Awad at Bethlehem Bible College. We had tea together and then we took him to see Hope School. From then on he sponsored a Hope School student and supported the Bible College. His own book, "God's Smuggler" had helped me in my Christian walk. Would he be willing though to write a foreword for my book? I hesitated and hesitated but finally put pen to paper to ask him. Back came the reply. He would be very pleased to be a part of my mission.

The week before Christmas I was out shopping when I met another member of St Matthews congregation, Janet Lunt. We stopped for a chat and she told me she had just been to collect her Christmas cards from the printers, she had designed them herself. I asked if I could have a peep — immediately I saw one, I knew that was the design I wanted for my book cover and after a visit with Janet she agreed I could use one of her drawings.

A whole new world was openig up for me. It was all coming together with very little effort on my part. There has been lots of new and interesting things to learn and see, like three special days in Bournemouth with Anne attending the Christian Booksellers Conference.

So what of the future? My season of rest is accomplishing its work, physically and psychologically. The book is now written and awaits printing and promoting. Ten per cent of the income from the sale of this book will go to the Hope Christian Trust, to be used for ministries in the Middle East. After that, only the Lord knows.

What I know is that, in the words of the hymn, Now thank we all our God:

He, Who from my mother's arms has blessed me on my way
with countless gifts of love...
is still mine today and will...
All my life be near me and that He will keep me in His grace
and guide me when perplexed and free me from all ills
in this world and the next...

Lynn Weaver
Bristol — July 1993

EPILOGUE

Shortly after finishing the manuscript of "Who From Our Mother's Arms" Lynn Weaver received a fresh and clear call to return to Bethlehem to minister for God in a new way.

Early in 1994 she plans to return to the Holy Land to act as the Public Relations Co-ordinator at the Bethlehem Bible College, under the auspices of The Hope Christian Trust. The Trust has a particular and special prayerful interest in the Palestinian Church on Israel's West Bank and in Gaza. It also seeks to actively support ministries working for reconciliation between Arab and Jewish Christian communities and was established specifically to support and encourage the indigenous church in Middle Eastern countries.

The Hope Christian Trust is developing its work in the following ways:—

1. By encouraging visitors and pilgrims to the Holy Land to visit Christian communities and meet local believers. It is making such a link-up possible through its own local contacts and Lynn will be involved in this.

2. By encouraging Christians in the United Kingdom to understand the situation in the Middle East and to intelligently pray "for the peace of Jerusalem". It distributes prayer letters and information as the needs arise.

3. By encouraging Christians to show active love and practical concern for their brothers and sisters in Christ, many of whom are in tough and difficult situations and sometimes persecuted because of their faith. It receives gifts and covenants for distribution in support of Christian activities and in response to known needs.

If you would like further details of how you can become involved with the work of the Trust or in supporting Lynn and the ministry of the Bethlehem Bible College please contact in England:—

John & Janet Angle,
19, Pyne Point,
Clevedon, Avon. BS21 7RL.
Tel/Fax 0275 872630